M

FOR YOUR READY REFERENCE

You will find in the following alphabetical lists:

1. Page numbers of songs appearing in both the pupils' books ("I Like the Country" and "I Like the City") and this Teacher's Book One ("Music Through the Day").
2. Songs recorded from "I Like the Country" and "I Like the City."
3. Songs recorded in this Teacher's Book One not appearing in the two pupils' books.

    (Songs recorded are indicated throughout this book by the symbol ® appearing, on the left, under the last staff of music.)

All albums for MUSIC FOR LIVING may be purchased directly from Silver Burdett Company. Albums may be purchased singly (one record each), or with the purchase of the set of 10 albums (of songs from "I Like the Country," "I Like the City" and Teacher's Book One), a convenient filing box will be supplied.

MUSIC FOR LIVING

THROUGH THE DAY

Music

Teacher's Book One

for Living

Through the Day

JAMES L. MURSELL

GLADYS TIPTON

BEATRICE LANDECK

HARRIET NORDHOLM

ROY E. FREEBURG

JACK M. WATSON

Illustrated by FEODOR ROJANKOVSKY

SILVER BURDETT COMPANY

Morristown, N. J. *New York* *Chicago* *San Francisco* *Dallas* *Atlanta*

Acknowledgments

It Is Our Credo that music can and should be a precious and potent influence for the development—personal, emotional, social—of children and young people. Certainly music should be presented in terms of the ways in which children learn. But, beyond this, musical experiences should help children towards a growing realization of the basic meanings and values of living. This is our united conviction and it has been our guiding thought in preparing these books.

In acting upon this belief we have found ourselves drawing upon the contributions of a host of persons. To all such we are conscious of deep indebtedness.

A great many composers, poets, and folklorists, through their creative achievements, have provided the songs and musical selections that are the materials of our books. A multitude of scholars and research workers have clarified the problems of child development, curriculum construction, and teaching procedures, and of the social significance of music itself. Their findings have guided us at every turn. To all such, living and dead, we authors and our publisher have the duty and privilege of expressing our gratitude.

But also there are many who have directly aided us in our undertaking, and more particularly with this first book of our series. Some have helped us primarily with the problems of music and music education, others in connection with related but more general issues. To all of them we wish, in this place, to give credit and convey our real gratitude.

The following music consultants have given us invaluable assistance in selecting and evaluating material: Evelyn H. Hunt (New York City), Dorothy G. Kelley (Indiana University), Ruth Liebers (New York City), Mildred McGowan (Los Angeles, California), Minerva Pepinsky (Northern Illinois State Teachers College), Helen Rothgeb (Bloomington, Illinois), Irene L. Schoepfle (Orange County, California), Madeline Siemann (New York City).

Other teachers and specialists in the field of music who have provided many useful suggestions are Maxine Blackwell (Kernersville, North Carolina), Lillian K. Boyce (El Centro, California), Ronald C. Cook (Fresno County, California), Alta B. Clark (Oneonta, California), Ralph Hess (Phoenix, Arizona), Pauline Judah (Columbus, Indiana), Adeline McCall (Chapel Hill, North Carolina), Lois Olsen (South Pasadena, California), Inez Rowzey (Los Angeles, California).

Our controlling viewpoint clearly implies that music should be brought into relationship with a wide range of experience and be treated as an integral element in general education. In developing this belief we have had valuable assistance from Ruth Zimmerman (Children's Librarian, Illinois State Normal University).

To all of these who have helped us with our work we tender our warm and sincere thanks.

The Authors

Contents

SINGING TIME
I wake in the morning early,
And always the very first thing,
I poke out my head
And I sit up in bed
And I sing and I sing and sing!
                    —ROSE FYLEMAN

v

Credits

Grateful acknowledgment is made to the following publishers, folklorists, and poets for the use of their material. If we have omitted any names, we trust we may be forgiven, as we have made every effort to locate all copyright owners.

Marion Abeson for the lyrics of "Giddy-ap Pony" from "Who Wants a Ride," Young People's Record 806.

The University of Alabama Press for "Picking Up Song" ("Little Bitty Man"), "Feeding Time" ("Little Girl"), "Going to the Lumberyard" ("Remember Me"), and "Little White Daisies"; also for "Hickety Pickety," "O My Little Boy," and "The Garden Wall" ("Roun' the Wall"). These songs are from the publication ALABAMA FOLK SONGS.

Marie Louise Allen for her poem, "The Mitten Song."

Byron Arnold for Alabama folk songs from his collection: "Frog in the Millpond," "The Old Gray Cat," and "Boil the Cabbage Down."

Associated Music Publishers, Inc., for "Sleighride" ("Schlittenfahrt"), from WINTERBILDERN by Zilcher. Copyright 1927, 1955, by Breitkopf and Härtel, Leipzig.

Augener Ltd., for "Jacky Stand Still" and "All the Ducks," from OLD DUTCH NURSERY RHYMES, English translation by R. H. Elkin.

Estate of Bela Bartok for PIANO PIECES FOR CHILDREN, Vol. 1, No. 10.

Dorothy Baruch for the poem "The Lawn Mower" from I LIKE MACHINERY, Harper & Brothers.

Estate of Lady Bell for the following songs from THE SINGING CIRCLE, Longmans Green & Co. Ltd.: "Who Will Come With Me," "Morning on the Farm," "The Cat in the Snow," and the tune of "Diddle-dy Diddle-dy."

Boosey and Hawkes, Inc., for "Arran Boat Song," from FOLK SONGS OF THE BRITISH ISLES, published in 1947 by Boosey and Hawkes.

Polly Chase Boyden for her poem, "Mud."

Broadcast Music Inc., New York, for "Big Bass Drum" from SONGS CHILDREN LOVE TO SING, arranged by Albert E. Wier; copyright 1916 by D. Appleton & Co., assigned to Broadcast Music Inc., New York, N. Y., 1944.

Marchette Chute for the poem, "Sliding," from RHYMES ABOUT THE CITY, published by The Macmillan Company.

Cincinnati Public Schools for "The Hat Man" from The New Primary Manual.

Cooperative Rec. Service for "I Want To Be a Farmer."

J. Curwen & Sons Ltd. for "Thankfulness," from GRADED ROUNDS AND CATCHES, Curwen Ed. 6079.

The John Day Company Inc. for the following material: the poem, "Stop-Go," from I LIKE AUTOMOBILES, copyright 1931 by Dorothy Walter Baruch; "My Tambourine" and "Merry Bells of Christmas Ring," from SINGING TIME, copyright 1929 by Satis N. Coleman and Alice G. Thorn; and "Let's Go Walking" and the melody of "Singing Time," from ANOTHER SINGING TIME, copyright 1937.

Katherine Dent for the poem, "Jigglity-Jogglety."

Estate of Edna Potter Divine for "Charlie Over the Water" from THIS WAY AND THAT, Oxford University Press.

E. P. Dutton & Co., Inc. for the poems "Jump or Jiggle," "The Seesaw," and "Work Horses," from ANOTHER HERE AND NOW STORY BOOK by Lucy Sprague Mitchell and co-authors. Copyright 1937 by E. P. Dutton & Co., Inc.

Eleanor Farjeon for "Down, Down" and "Music" ("Hurdy-Gurdy"), both from POEMS FOR CHILDREN, published by J. B. Lippincott Co.

Carl Fischer, Inc. for "The Egg," from TWELVE FOLK SONGS BY JOHANNES BRAHMS, arranged by Guy Maier.

Folkways Records & Service Corp. for "Watch That Lady" and "Upstairs and Down."

Harper & Brothers for the poem, "The Turtle," from I KNOW SOME LITTLE ANIMALS by James S. Tippett. Copyright 1941 by Harper & Brothers. Also for the poem, "In the City," from I LIVE IN A CITY by James S. Tippett. Copyright 1927 by Harper & Brothers..

D. C. Heath and Company for the poem, "Roadways," by Lucy Sprague Mitchell, from OUR COUNTRY.

Henry Holt and Company, Inc. for "The Cupboard" from COLLECTED POEMS by Walter de la Mare. Copyright 1920 by Henry Holt and Company, Inc. Copyright 1948 by Walter de la Mare. Public performance of this poem has to be cleared with Holt.

Jewish Education Committee of New York, Inc., for "On This Night" by S. E. Goldfarb and S. S. Grossman.

Laidlaw Brothers Incorporated for "The Bear," from PLAY SONGS by Alys Bentley.

Leeds Music Corporation for "A Little Joke," by Kabalevsky, and "Tarantelle," Op. 65, by Prokofieff.

Liveright Publishing Corporation for "Hayride," from PLAYTIME WITH MUSIC by Abeson and Bailey.

Ruby Terrill Lomax for "Ha, Ha! This-a-way" from NEGRO FOLK SONGS AS SUNG BY LEADBELLY; and "Little Bird, Go Through My Window" and "The Wind Blew East" from OUR SINGING COUNTRY, published by The Macmillan Co.

Flora McDowell for "I Belong to That Band" and "Mothers Make a Home." SONGS OF THE OLD CAMP GROUND.

The Macmillan Company, for "Hello, Somebody" from SHANTY MEN AND SHANTY BOYS by William Doerflinger.

Edward B. Marks Music Corporation for "O Christmas Tree" from SONGS TO GROW ON.

William A. Owens for "Tideo" and "The Cymbals" from SWING AND TURN, Tardy Publishing Company.

Pantheon Books Inc. for "Now It Is Christmas" from THE TRAPP FAMILY BOOK OF CHRISTMAS SONGS.

The Pennsylvania Dutch Folklore Center, Inc., for "Joe Rattle" from SONGS ALONG THE MAHANTONGO.

Theodore Presser Co., copyright owner, for "When the Train Comes Along," from AMERICAN NEGRO SONGS by John W. Work.

Proprietors of Hymns Ancient and Modern, for "Christmas Chant" ("A Solis Ortus Cardine"), from A PLAINSONG HYMN BOOK.

G. P. Putnam's Sons for the following poems by Dorothy Aldis: "The Seals" and "In the Barnyard" from HOP, SKIP, AND JUMP; "Like Me" and "Singing" from A CHILD'S TREASURY OF VERSE; "All a Duck Needs" and "Hungry Waves" (adapted) from HERE, THERE, AND EVERYWHERE; and "Gayest of All" from BEFORE THINGS HAPPEN.

G. Schirmer, Inc. for lyrics of "Mr. Turkey," from BARNYARD BALLADS FOR CHILDREN by Anice Terhune. Copyright 1910 by G. Schirmer, Inc.

B. Schott's Soehne, Mainz (courtesy of Associated Music Publishers, Inc., New York), and Alexander Gretchaninoff, for "Out for a Walk" ("A La Promenade"), from GRANDFATHER'S BOOK, Op. 119.

The Society of Authors for permission to use Rose Fyleman's poem, "Singing Time," in musical setting.

Janet Tobitt for "I Got Bananas." BOOK OF NEGRO SONGS.

Henri Wehrmann for "Compèr Lapin" ("The Rabbit") from CREOLE SONGS OF THE DEEP SOUTH.

Young People's Records for the tune of "Giddy-ap Pony" from "Who Wants a Ride," Record No. 806.

Getting Acquainted

1

When a child first comes to school, he has a great deal of getting acquainted to do—with teacher, with other children and, in a very real sense, with himself. Since music can be a real help with all this, he needs to get acquainted with music, too. So this book is begun with a chapter of introductions. Personalize the songs freely, by using names of children, greetings, references to familiar things; by changing words to fit the occasion or making up entirely new words. Many songs in this book lend themselves to such treatment. It will help to make the child feel confident generally and will put him on easy terms with singing. Rhythmic movement comes natural to children. Stress on this valuable phase of musical development can do much to put them at their ease. Use both large movements and small ones (fingers, hands, etc.). Many songs, piano selections, and records will be useful. Simple instruments can help, too. To avoid confusion, introduce one at a time.

One misty, moisty morning,
When cloudy was the weather,
I chanced to meet an old man
Clad all in leather.
He began to compliment;
I began to grin;
How do you do?
And how do you do?
And how do you do again?

—*Mother Goose*

Every child feels like "somebody," especially on that big first day of school. So it's important to have a "Hello, Somebody" song that helps everyone to get acquainted. Later, when the first strangeness has worn off, each child will want to sing his name as the group sings "Somebody wants to know your name" to each in turn.

Hello, Somebody

ENGLISH SEA CHANTEY

Many "somebodies" have called this song their own—have used it in ways that fitted the pattern of their everydays. The version printed above went out to sea, where it gradually accumulated many different verses as the chanteyman sought to keep the sailors amused while they hoisted topgallant sails. The men worked to the rhythm of the song and joined in the chorus, "Hello, Somebody, hello." This interpolated unison chorus is the essential character of this song. So long as we retain this character, we too may invent new verses describing the many different things our "Somebodies" want to do.

2

The Little White Daisies

FOLK SONG FROM ALABAMA

Use of a child's name in a song builds self-confi-
dence, helps him to join his group. On birthdays
we use this song to sing, "This is Johnny's birthday;
he's six years old today," etc.

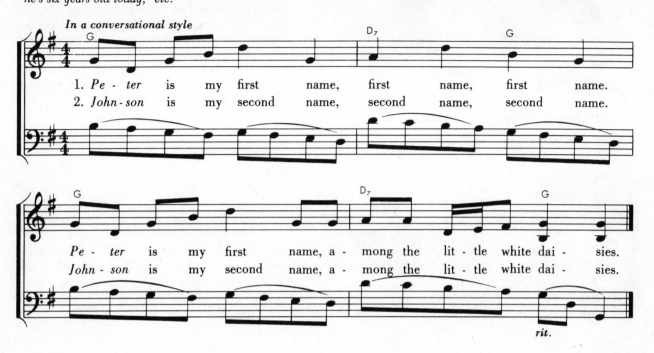

1. Pe - ter is my first name, first name, first name.
2. John - son is my second name, second name, second name.

Pe - ter is my first name, a - mong the lit - tle white dai - sies.
John - son is my second name, a - mong the lit - tle white dai - sies.

Who Are You?

WORDS ADAPTED
GERMAN MELODY

Your Sallys and Sues will gladly accept an invita-
tion to sing their names in verse 2. Some names
fit better than others. Who cares? What matters is
that Sue sings alone, without embarrassment.

1. A lit - tle {boy/girl} went walk - ing by, walk - ing by, walk - ing by, A
2. "My name is Sal - ly An - der - son, An - der - son, An - der - son, My

lit - tle {boy/girl} went walk - ing by. {"Who are you?"/"How are you?"}
name is Sal - ly An - der - son, How do you do?"

3

Hand games are fun and good practice, too, in small muscle co-ordination. Teacher will not be surprised if all her children do not react to the music in the same way and at the same time. She knows that since six-year-olds are literally pioneering all these new pathways with their muscles, they need time to develop control.

Put Your Finger in the Air

WORDS AND MUSIC BY WOODY GUTHRIE

3. Put your finger on your nose,
   And feel how the cold wind blows,

4. Put your finger on your shoe,
   And leave it a day or two,

5. Put your finger on your finger,
   And your finger on your finger,

6. Put your finger on your chin,
   That's where the food slips in,

7. Put your finger on your cheek,
   And leave it about a week,

It's fun to punctuate the day with movement to music. After years of free play at home, most children find it a strain to sit still too long.

WORDS PARAPHRASED BY LOUISE KESSLER
DANISH FOLK SONG

Vigorously

I trav-eled far a-cross the sea, I met a man and old was he. "Old man," I said, "Where do you live?" And this is what he told me.

1. "Fol-low me to Stamp-ing Land, Stamp-ing Land, Stamp-ing Land,
2. "Fol-low me to Clap-ping Land, Clap-ping Land, Clap-ping Land,

All who wish to live with me, Fol-low me to Stamp-ing Land."
All who wish to live with me, Fol-low me to Clap-ping Land."

There are many lands to which it is fun to go with this song. The children will enjoy helping to make plans. Just to get the suitcase a-packing, here are a few ideas:

Pointing land,	Nodding land,
Skipping land,	Tapping land.
Hopping (on one leg) land,	

MUSIC FOR LIVING RECORDS, available from the publisher, include 62 songs from *Through the Day*. Each song recorded is indicated by the symbol ® appearing, on the left, under the last staff of music.

5

Ha, Ha, This-a-way

GAME SONG

Each boy and girl will want a turn at being the "leader" who thinks of some interesting motion for the others to follow. Teacher may help a shy child be a good leader and thus win respect.

{Ha, ha,} {Hi, hi,} {Ho, ho,} this - a - way, {Ha, ha,} {Hi, hi,} {Ho, ho,} that - a - way, {Ha, ha,} {Hi, hi,} {Ho, ho,} this - a - way,

Then, oh, then. When I was a lit - tle {boy,} {girl,} Lit - tle {boy,} {girl,} lit - tle {boy,} {girl,}

When I was a lit - tle {boy,} {girl,} Six years old.

As this song becomes familiar, it may be used as a musical conversation. All sing as far as "then" with the soloist, who makes a verse reporting summer activities:

> I went swimming, swimming, swimming,
> I went swimming every day.

Or I saw the circus, circus, circus,
I saw the circus in the big tent.

Later in the year various activities may be sung about and dramatized:

> When I was a carpenter, carpenter, carpenter, (or fireman, etc.)
> When I was a carpenter I worked like this.

Seasonal activities need discussion, too:

> I saw a robin, a robin, a robin,
> I saw a robin in the grass.

Or Christmas is coming, coming, coming,
Christmas is coming right away.

Six-year-olds need no urging to rhythmic activities. Exploring a run, for instance, seems almost second nature: "How many ways can I run?" "I'm a squirrel—a jet plane." "I'm running to meet Daddy." And with each new characterization, the run takes on a different quality of expressiveness.

What Shall We Do?

GAME SONG

Brightly

1. What shall we do when we all go out, All go out, all go out;
2. We will __ climb an __ ap - ple tree, ap - ple tree, ap - ple tree;

What shall we do when we all go out, When we all go out to play?
We will __ climb an __ ap - ple tree, When we all go out to play.

Dramatizing a song is a way for children to make it their own. Moving joyously and dramatically, their bodies absorb and express the rhythmic flow of the music. Role-playing helps them understand the words, so their minds are active too. Such experiences can help them live in their world. Verse 1 of this song invites children to sing of many things they can do when they "all go out to play." Endless stanzas will undoubtedly be made up as the children sing about and dramatize their real-life experiences, for in the words of James Stephens: "When I was young I dared to sing of anything and everything."

3. We will jump like jumping jacks,
   When we all go out to play.
4. We will play a game of tag,
5. We will ride our bikes around,
6. We will plant some flower seeds,
7. We will catch some lightning bugs,
8. We will go to the grocery store,
9. We will find some colored leaves,
10. We will make a big snowman,

7

Going to Boston

AMERICAN PLAY-PARTY SONG

We use this song to invite children to enjoy full body movement—perhaps an original dance. Boston sounds delightful at this "here and now" stage. What "six" gives a fig where it is?

8

Who Will Come with Me?

TRADITIONAL SONG

We serve our children best when our accompaniments pick up their own patterns and tempos. (Children's tempos are usually faster than adults.) Teacher needs to have an array of instruments.

Gaily

1. Who will come with me, the jol - ly, jol - ly rov - er?
2. Who will skip with me, the jol - ly, jol - ly rov - er?

Who will come with me, the jol - ly, jol - ly rov - er,
Who will skip with me, the jol - ly, jol - ly rov - er,

And see, _____ and see, _____ and see what we can see?
And see, _____ and see, _____ and see what we can see?

Parallel listening: "Skating," Kullak. RCA Victor Basic Library.

What does it matter if Johnny's run seems bumbling and awkward, as he reaches out with his body to catch the "feel" of a sea gull in flight? What he is doing is finding himself, rhythmically speaking. What he needs is to develop, rhythmically, in his own good time and in his particular way. As each child experiments, he develops his own unique movement patterns.

Who will skip with me?

Sally may choose to skip to this song.
On a tambourine we play: ♩ ♪♩ ♪♩| ♩.

Who will walk with me?

Peter would rather walk. A drum is good for walking: ♩ ♩ ♩ ♩| ♩.

Who will skate with me?

Sand blocks are fine: ♩ ♩♩ ♩ ♩♩ ♩.

9

Jim-Along Josie

FOLK SONG FROM NEW ENGLAND

Whether we skip or walk to this gay chorus, it's grand to hear the crash of a cymbal every time we sing the "Hi."

Hi, come a-long, Jim-a-long, Jo-sie! Hi, come a-long, Jim-a-long, Joe!

Hi, come a-long, Jim-a-long, Jo-sie! Hi, come a-long, Jim-a-long, Joe!

Tippy Tippy Tiptoe

WORDS ANONYMOUS
MUSIC BY MILTON KAYE

The fun of tiptoeing to this music is enhanced if there's a dramatic reason. Perhaps grandma is sleeping or there's a surprise for daddy. Use of finger cymbals adds to the music, too.

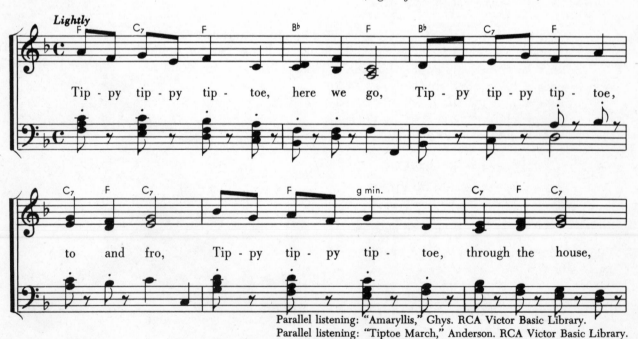

Tip-py tip-py tip-toe, here we go, Tip-py tip-py tip-toe,

to and fro, Tip-py tip-py tip-toe, through the house,

Parallel listening: "Amaryllis," Ghys. RCA Victor Basic Library.
Parallel listening: "Tiptoe March," Anderson. RCA Victor Basic Library.

10

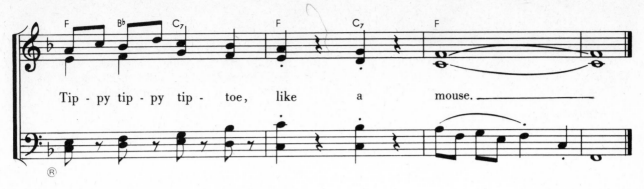

Tip - py tip - py tip - toe, like a mouse.

The song suggests "walking down the street," then skipping. Everybody skips! Some skip better than others, for co-ordination differs.

Rig-a-Jig-Jig

ENGLISH FOLK SONG

Briskly

As I was walk - ing down the street, Down the street, down the street, A

{ pret - ty girl / nice young man } I chanced to meet, Heigh - o, heigh - o, heigh - o.

Rig - a - jig - jig, and a - way we go, A - way we go, a - way we go;

Rig - a - jig - jig, and a - way we go, Heigh - o, heigh - o, heigh - o.

Fiddler, Play for Me

WORDS BY MARION EDEY
GERMAN FOLK SONG

Music is sometimes used by children to enhance an idea that has caught their fancy. John made some words for the interlude of this song, one day, and "solo dancing" soon turned into a group play.

1. Fid - dler, fid - dler, play for me, Make your fid - dle sing, sing!
2. Pus - sy cat will dance with you, Pus - sy's good at turn - ing.

Ev - 'ry boy and girl you see Dan - ces round the ring, ring.
I shall dance with Pus - sy, too, While our Pus - sy's learn - ing.

3. In and out and in and out,
Flying like a swallow.
Spin about and spin about,
Follow, follow, follow.

Rhythm instruments may be used or real instruments pantomimed:
"Fred will play the violin" or "John will play the kettledrums."

12

Some songs seem to pick up new verses naturally. "Toodala" has had many a pretty motion and countless new verses since the early days in Texas, when "Toodala" square dance parties were held out-of-doors, with whole families riding in from afar.

Toodala

PLAY-PARTY GAME FROM TEXAS

Easily

1. Might-y pret-ty mo-tion, too-da-la, too-da-la, too-da-la,
2. Rock __ old __ Son-i, too-da-la, too-da-la, too-da-la,

Might-y pret-ty mo-tion, too-da-la, too-da-la-la' la-dy.
Rock __ old __ Son-i, too-da-la, too-da-la-la la-dy.

From TOODALA by Helen Gates. Used by permission of the Texas Folklore Society.

"This dance song sings easily over and over without stopping—picking up whatever things are happening — noticing new toys, bright colors, the weather."* Commenting also on holidays as they come and go, and on the many patterns of movement into which little bodies are apt to fall. "Toodala" can also be used for a group undertaking later in the year.

Jumping up and down
Swimming in the pool

Making a snowman
Picking violets (dandelions, tulips, etc.)
Bouncing my ball

I'm a Jack-o'-lantern
Happy birthday, Johnny

Playing the drum
Playing rhythm sticks
(Try playing instruments on each "Toodala")

Toward the end of the year, teacher finds the tone for "lady" on the melody bells. Child plays tone when the word is sung in the song.

*Quoted from Ruth Seeger's invaluable AMERICAN FOLK SONGS FOR CHILDREN. Doubleday, 1948.

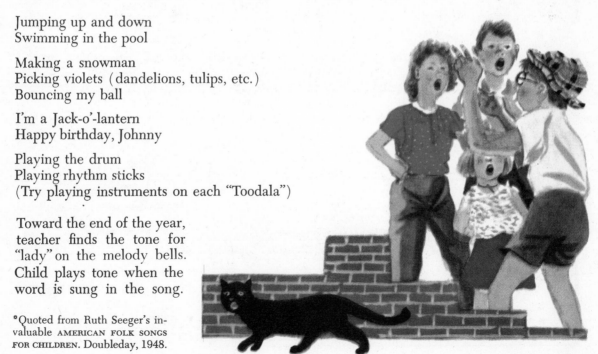

The joy that all children have in singing games is very useful to the teacher who is anxious to help her children solve individual problems that keep them from being part of the group. Barbara evidenced antagonism to her peers—until the day they sang, "Where, oh where, is dear little Barbara?" and hunted for her, while she hid.

The Pawpaw Patch

SINGING GAME FROM KENTUCKY

This is one of many songs teacher may use to make her day move more smoothly, more happily. "Where, oh where, is dear little Nancy?" With a merry smile she makes a joke of Nancy's reluctance to join the group.

Charlie over the Water

SINGING GAME

Children form a ring about "Charlie." On "me," all stoop as quickly as they can. Any child is "it" if "Charlie" catches him before he stoops. A good song, too, for playing a pitch game. One child sings alternate pitch (measure 4). Others guess.

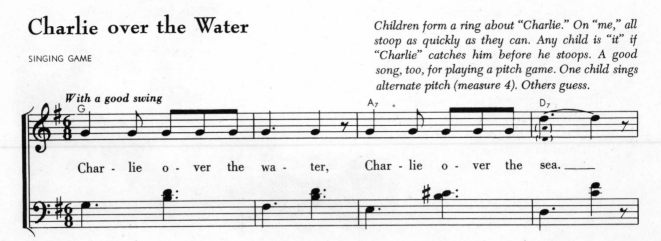

Char - lie caught a black - bird,* Might been me.

*Also "white fish" or "big whale" or whatever the children may suggest.

Children form a circle, joining hands to make "windows," thru which the "little birds" go.

Little Bird, Go Through My Window

SINGING GAME

1. Lit - tle bird, lit - tle bird, go through my win - dow, Lit - tle bird, lit - tle bird, go
2. Blue - bird, blue - bird, go through my win - dow, Blue - bird, blue - bird, go

through my win - dow, Lit - tle bird, lit - tle bird, go through my win - dow, And
through my win - dow, Blue - bird, blue - bird, go through my win - dow, And

Refrain

buy mo - las - ses can - dy. Go through my win - dow, my sug - ar lump, Go
buy mo - las - ses can - dy.

through my win - dow, my sug - ar lump, And buy mo - las - ses can - dy. dy.

15

Hickety Pickety

WORDS ADAPTED
ALABAMA FOLK SONG

1. Hick-et-y, pick-et-y, horn-y cup, Can you guess what I'm going to touch?
2. Hick-et-y, pick-et-y, horn-y aye, Can you guess what I'm going to play?

The ping of a water glass tapped by a pencil . . . the thump of a boot on the floor . . . these and all the sounds in our environment fascinate little children. To help little ears develop, we share their pleasure in all kinds of sound, point out that some sounds are more meaningful than others, and sharpen hearing with a guessing game:

1. Hickety, pickety, horny cup,
   Can you guess what I'm going to touch?

Children close eyes and guess as teacher (or, later, child) taps chair with pencil; taps radiator or makes some other sound.

2. Hickety, pickety, horny aye,
   Can you guess what I'm going to play?

*Musical instruments sing with many different kinds of voices.
Our children learn to identify the sound of piano . . triangle . . etc.*

3. Hickety, pickety, horny oh,
   Can you guess how my feet will go?

*Different kinds of movement create different kinds of rhythmic patterns.
Children identify a run, walk, slide or skate, hop or jump, skip or gallop,
from listening to the sound of footfalls on the floor.*

4. Hickety, pickety, horny pan,
   Can you guess who I am?

*Children listen to and recognize the subtle differences in the quality
of their friends' voices. Or they may sing, "Can you guess what I am?"
indicating a train with "Too-too," or a fire truck with "Whooooo."*

Jingle at the Window

TEXAS PLAY-PARTY GAME

Children walk about the room or around the circle with their instruments. At "Jingle at the window," they stop in place and jingle bells; shake tambourines, or ring triangles.

Briskly

Skip one win - dow, Ti - de - o,

Skip two win - dows, Ti - de - o, Skip three win - dows,

Ti - de - o, Jin - gle at the win - dows,

Ti - de - o. Jin - gling, jin - gling, jin - gling Joe,

Jin - gle at the win - dows, Ti - de - o.

The Cymbals

TEXAS PLAY-PARTY GAME

As we follow the suggestions given by the words of this song, we discover that the cymbals are capable of giving different kinds of sound effects.

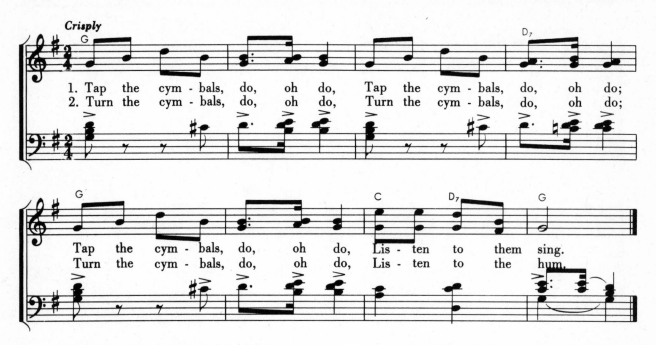

1. Tap the cym - bals, do, oh do, Tap the cym - bals, do, oh do;
2. Turn the cym - bals, do, oh do, Turn the cym - bals, do, oh do;

Tap the cym - bals, do, oh do, Lis - ten to them sing.
Turn the cym - bals, do, oh do, Lis - ten to the hum.

3. Clap the cymbals, do, oh do,
   Listen to them ring.

My Tambourine

WORDS AND MUSIC BY SATIS COLEMAN

The words of a song sometimes help in discovering the resources of an instrument and how to play it. In this song the music helps, too, since it is written in a real tambourine rhythm.

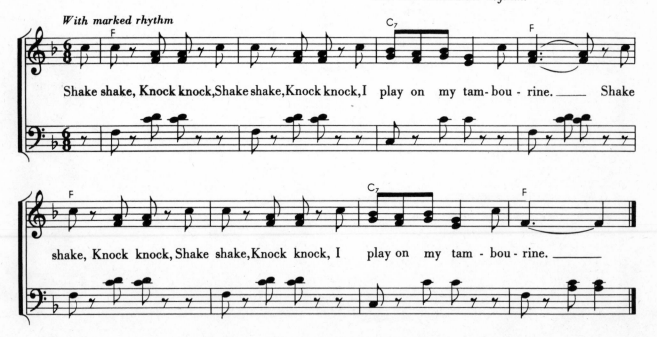

Shake shake, Knock knock, Shake shake, Knock knock, I play on my tam-bou - rine.____ Shake

shake, Knock knock, Shake shake, Knock knock, I play on my tam - bou - rine. ____

18

Orchestra Song

Grown-ups' instruments are fun, too, particularly if we invite parents or uppergraders to bring them to the first-grade room where they can play them for us and let us handle them.

WORDS PARAPHRASED BY MARIE LOUISE ALLEN
GERMAN FOLK SONG

1. What kind of a song does my fid-dle sing? Fee-lee-fee-lee-fee, Fee-lee-fee-lee-fee, Hear my fid-dle sing-ing.
2. What kind of a song does my trum-pet sing? Tah-tah-rah-tah-tah, Tah-tah-rah-tah-tah, Hear my trum-pet sing-ing.

Flute: Hoo-lee-hoo-lee-hoo
Clarinet: Doo-dle-doo-dle-det
Mandolin: Bleng-a-bleng-a-bleng
Bass viol: Shroom-shroom-shroom
Harp: Plink-plink-plink
Tuba: Boop-boop-boop
Trombone: Toom-pa-toom-pa-toom
Bass drum: Boom-boom-boom

Twinkle, Twinkle, Little Star

OLD RHYME
FRENCH FOLK SONG

The sound of a triangle seems to twinkle, doesn't it? Finger cymbals are appropriate, too. By following the rhythm of the words, children can avoid trouble with the long notes. Try, also, playing this tune by ear on the piano or bells.

Twin - kle, twin - kle, lit - tle star, How I won - der what you are.

Up a - bove the world so high, Like a dia - mond in the sky.

Twin - kle, twin - kle, lit - tle star, How I won - der what you are.

Parallel listening: "Dance of the Sugar Plum Fairy," from *Nutcracker Suite*, Tchaikovsky.

The above tune may be used for this hand play or song-story for dramatizing:
Once there were two blackbirds sitting on a hill,
One named Jack, the other named Jill.
Fly away, Jack; Fly away, Jill;
Come back, Jack; Come back, Jill.

Big Bass Drum

WORDS AND MUSIC ANONYMOUS

The strong accents in this song will suggest a drum and also how to play it.

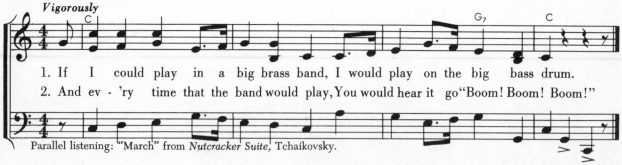

1. If I could play in a big brass band, I would play on the big bass drum.
2. And ev - 'ry time that the band would play, You would hear it go "Boom! Boom! Boom!"

Parallel listening: "March" from *Nutcracker Suite*, Tchaikovsky.

The playing of instruments may be combined with dramatization. Some children will enjoy acting out this song while others play instruments.

MOTHER GOOSE RHYME
MUSIC BY J. W. ELLIOTT

With an easy swing

Hick - o - ry, dick - o - ry, dock, The mouse ran up the clock; The clock struck one, The mouse ran down; Hick - o - ry, dick - o - ry, dock.

Parallel listening: "Mother Goose Songs" sung by Burl Ives. Columbia.
Parallel listening: "Mother Goose Songs" sung by Frank Luther. Decca.

"How can we make a sound like the ticking of a clock?" Some may tap a chair with a pencil. Others may think of their rhythm sticks or wood blocks. Sally finds that tapping the chair seat and rung alternately produces a real "tick tock" sound. Joe finds that tapping a small, then a larger block gives a like effect, and is easier. "Who would like to be the pendulum of this big clock?" There are many ways to play at being pendulum:

Heads nodding from side to side,
One arm swinging, with clasped hands,
Both arms swinging, with clasped hands,
Arm bent at elbow, swinging back and forth,
Swinging upper body (feet well apart).

The children also find ways to dramatize the striking of the clock. Some may clap. Others may think the triangle gives just the right kind of chiming sound. Still others may prefer a cymbal clap. It is fun, too, to describe the mouse as he runs up and down the clock by playing a glissando first up and then down on the piano or on the melody bells.

21

I Belong to That Band

CAMP MEETING SONG

When teacher starts singing this song, Tom and Sue and "all God's children" come running to join the band, eager to play an instrument and help decide which one is best for playing the "hallelus."

All the broth-ers want to go, Why_ don't they come a - long?_ I be- long_to that band, hal-le-lu! Hal- le - lu - jah! Hal- le- lu - jah! I be-long_to that band, hal-le-lu! ___

A Play Song

WORDS AND MUSIC BY CLARA ELLEN SPELMAN

We may also sing "who likes to work," showing, in the places where the song has no words, how we pound or chop or saw.

Once there was a {boy}{girl} who liked to play. (Hum, play melody bells, or make up words to sing)

Ev- 'ry - one would say,"How {he}{she} likes to play."

Among the instruments "we like to play" are the melody bells. Children may play the actual pitches of this song, since they are simple and scalewise—or they may like to sing the song several times, adding two rhythm instruments each time. Another interesting plan is to use ringing or jingling instruments for measures 3 and 4 and contrasting, tapping instruments for 7 and 8.

22

Regular rhythmic patterns are often set up by work motions (sawing) or play motions (patting clay). As these are repeated over and over, they sometimes prompt spontaneous, almost unconscious song, since music has recurring rhythmic patterns, too. Movement carried along on a tune is steadied, made more efficient, since strain is alleviated.

Picking Up Song

FOLK SONG FROM ALABAMA

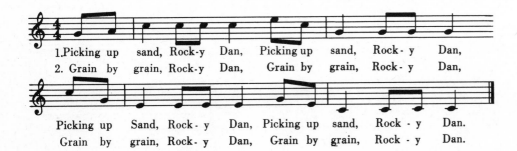

Any time in the day is a good time to have music that arises spontaneously, that really fills a need. Anything done to music is done in a relaxed and happy way. Teacher gets what she wants the easy way when she sings, "Pick up your coat, Johnny boy," to the tune of the "Picking Up Song." Children are quick to respond, "Picking up coats, one by one" . . . or blocks, or paper, or what have you?

Children are delighted when teacher surprises them with a sung, instead of a spoken, "Good morning." The tune that comes to mind may not be immortal. No matter. When teacher is free and easy with a tune, children readily sing answers to musical questions:

Musical Questions

WORDS AND MUSIC BY GRACE M. MESERVE

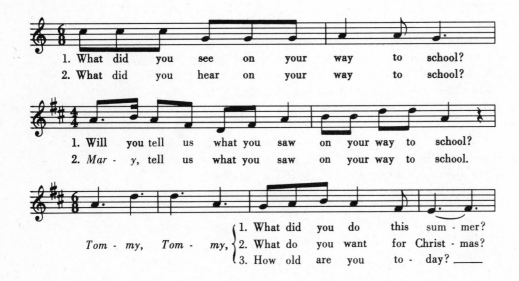

A Work Chant

WORDS BY V. S. BURRINGTON
FRENCH NURSERY TUNE

When people are happily excited, their voices are apt to rise in pitch. Raising the pitch of a song lends zest and variety to frequent repetition.

This little work chant may free children to make other chants—all their own. Children chant naturally as they play freely—until something happens to inhibit them. A child chanting softly to himself need not disturb his fellows. Rather his quiet satisfaction is apt to be infectious, relaxing, and cheering to his entire group.

Children are fascinated by the sound of their names. A name sounded over and over makes a pleasantly rhythmical chant. Sometimes a tune will "happen," sometimes not; but rhythmic movement grows very naturally out of such a chant. Thus "Barbara" may suggest skipping or sliding; "John, John, John" may turn into a march or hop. Chanting, moving, clapping a name, and finally choosing the instrument for accompaniment, contribute both to personal status and musical satisfaction.

24

Home Sweet Home

2

Mothers Make a Home

RELIGIOUS FOLK SONG FROM TENNESSEE

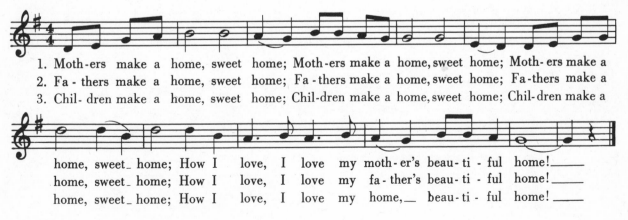

1. Moth-ers make a home, sweet home; Moth-ers make a home, sweet home; Moth-ers make a
2. Fa-thers make a home, sweet home; Fa-thers make a home, sweet home; Fa-thers make a
3. Chil-dren make a home, sweet home; Chil-dren make a home, sweet home; Chil-dren make a

home, sweet home; How I love, I love my moth-er's beau-ti-ful home!____
home, sweet home; How I love, I love my fa-ther's beau-ti-ful home!____
home, sweet home; How I love, I love my home,__ beau-ti-ful home!____

When daddy walks with Jean and me,
We have a lot of fun,
'Cause we can't walk as fast as he,
Unless we skip and run!

I stretch and stretch my legs so far,
I nearly slip and fall,
But how does daddy take such steps?
He doesn't stretch at all!

—GRACE GLAUBITZ

Each person's "self" is something individual, yet it has a social origin, since most of us think of ourselves in terms of what others think and feel about us. This is particularly true of a child's early self-appraisal during his first years at school. The thoughtful teacher helps each child find his real self, accept it, and be true to it.

I Have a Bonnet

FOLK SONG FROM IRELAND
COLLECTED BY JEAN RITCHIE

1. I have a bon-net trimmed with blue. Why don't you wear it? So I do.
2. I have a bon-net trimmed with blue. Listen to the mu-sic play for you!

I have a bon-net trimmed with blue. Why don't you wear it? So I do.
I have a bon-net trimmed with blue. Listen to the mu-sic play for you!

I will wear it when I can, When I go out with a fair-haired man,
I have a bon-net trimmed with blue. Why don't you wear it? So I do.

I will wear it when I can, When I go out with a fair-haired man.
I have a bon-net trimmed with blue. Why don't you wear it? So I do.

Here is a song for Hetty and Johnny and Mary and all the "me's" in the classroom, and a way to compliment them when they look nice or do something well, e.g., "Whenever Susie paints a nice picture . . ."

The Green Dress

TRANSLATED BY JOSEF MARAIS
FOLK SONG FROM SOUTH AFRICA

When-ev-er Het-ty puts a green dress on, green dress on,

green dress on, When-ev-er Het-ty puts a green dress on,

I will sing a song for her. Let us sing a song, it

need-n't be so long, my Het-ty has a green dress on. on.

Birthday Song

WORDS BY EVELYN H. HUNT
SPIRITUAL

A birthday is the one big day of the year on which each "self" shines—and shines alone. Thus, no birthday goes unheeded by a teacher anxious to help her children find themselves.

{Mar - y's / George is} six years old to - day, {Mar - y's / George is} six years old to - day. Oh, {she / he} feels so hap - py in {her / his} heart, 'Cause {she's / he's} six years old to - day.

Children sit in circle outlining a big cake. Six stand in center, representing candles on cake. When the birthday person "blows them out," they sit, one by one.

Did You See My Man?

FOLK SONG FROM IRELAND
COLLECTED BY JEAN RITCHIE

This "dandling" song comes from the home, where it was sung as babies were bounced up and down on the knee, or given a ride on daddy's foot. Dolls and Teddy bears take the place of "baby" for six-year-olds.

1. Oh, did you see my man, he was a fine man,
2. He wore a blue jacket, a pair of white socks, A

Did you see my man look - ing for me? } And did you see my man,
hat on his head and a pail in his hand,

28

he was a fine man, Did you see my man look-ing for me?

Because the words of this song are full of repetition, it is an easy one to adapt. One nice plan is to offer children an opportunity to gain self-confidence by singing an answer to some easy question.

O My Little Boy

FOLK SONG FROM ALABAMA

O my lit - tle boy, who made your brit - ches? O my lit - tle boy,

who made your brit - ches? O my lit - tle boy, who made your brit - ches?

Mom - my cut 'em out and Dad - dy sewed the stit - ches.

"O my little girl, who braids your pigtails?"
"Mamma braids the braids and daddy ties the ribbon."

"O my little boy, who tied your shoelace?"
"I can tie my own, and no one needs to help me."

29

Telephone Song

WORDS AND MUSIC BY ERNEST GOLD

Crisply

The tel - e - phone sleeps most of the day, But when it wakes up you can

hear it say: "Ling-a-ling-a-ling-a-ling, ling-a-ling-a-ling-a-ling!"

Can you hear the tel - e - phone ring? "Ling - a - ling - a - ling - a - ling,

ling - a - ling - a - ling - a - ling!" I can hear the tel - e - phone ring.

℗ Parallel listening: "Lonesome House." Children's Record Guild.

30

The Cupboard

WORDS BY WALTER DE LA MARE
MUSIC BY ARTHUR EDWARDS

Maybe there's a box of cookies or a great big chocolate bar behind that key. Each child will enjoy singing about what he likes best of all.

Lively

I know a lit-tle cup-board with a tee-ny ti-ny key, And there's a jar of lol-li-pops for me, me, me.

Melody

31

Boil the Cabbage Down

FOLK SONG FROM ALABAMA

This old fiddle tune is a good recipe for just about any cooking that needs to be done.

1. Boil the cab - bage down,   Boil the cab - bage down,
2. Bake the bis - cuits brown,   Bake the bis - cuits brown,

All in the world that I can sing Is to boil the cab - bage down.
All in the world that I can sing Is to bake the bis - cuits brown.

3. Mix the cookies now,
4. Roll the cookies now,
5. Cut the cookies now,
6. Slide them in the oven,
7. Bake the cookies brown.

Mix a Pancake

WORDS BY CHRISTINA ROSSETTI
MUSIC BY ERNEST GOLD

As for the eating—sing, "Butter on the pancake, Yum, yum, yum," to "Skip to My Lou."(See p.68.)

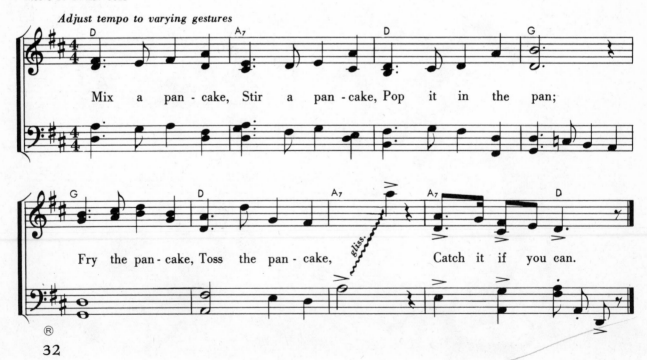

Mix a pan - cake, Stir a pan - cake, Pop it in the pan;

Fry the pan - cake, Toss the pan - cake, Catch it if you can.

*All of which goes to show that life is really as full
of ups and downs as is this "up and down" tune.*

Upstairs and Down

CHILDREN'S STREET GAME
COLLECTED BY TONY SCHWARTZ

Gleefully

I went up-stairs to make my bed, and
by mis-take I bumped my head. I went down-stairs to
cook my food, and by mis-take I cooked my shoe.

See Folkways Record FP 703, "1, 2, 3 and a Zing Zing Zing."

*We may put the kettle on for lunch or for a party
for our dolls. Or we may sing, "Bobby put your
rubbers on, We're going home."*

Polly, Put the Kettle On

ENGLISH NURSERY RHYME
SCOTTISH TUNE

Brightly

1. Pol - ly, put the ket - tle on, Pol - ly, put the ket - tle on,
2. Slice the bread and but - ter fine, Slice the bread and but - ter fine,

Pol - ly, put the ket - tle on, We'll all have tea.
Slice e - nough for eight or nine, We'll all have tea.

Parallel listening: "Polly, Put the Kettle On" (English). RCA Victor Basic Library.

3. Now mix up the ginger cake, (2 times)
   Stir the fire and let it bake,

4. Put the muffins in to roast, (2 times)
   Spread some jelly on the toast,

5. Johnny, set the table now, (2 times)
   Put the dishes in a row,

6. Pass around the pumpkin pie, (2 times)
   And the fritters made of rye,

33

Fais do do

WORDS PARAPHRASED BY ELEANOR GRAHAM VANCE
FRENCH NURSERY SONG

The title of this song means "Go to sleep." It is nice to sing these words in French at the beginning of each verse. The pronunciation is simple—fay doh-doh.

1. Go to sleep, my dear lit-tle sis-ter. Close your eyes and go__ to sleep. You'll find a sur-prise When you are a-wake, For Moth-er is bus-y Mak-ing a cake.

2. Go to sleep, my dear lit-tle broth-er. Close your eyes and go__ to sleep. When Dad-dy comes home, He'll make you a boat. When you have your bath, We'll set it a-float.

3. Go to sleep, my dear lit-tle ted-dy. Close your eyes and go__ to sleep. I'll put a soft pil-low Un-der your head, And I'll keep you warm Right here in my bed.

34

All Night, All Day

SPIRITUAL

"Angels watching over me," and loving parents too—such thoughts make a child feel secure. "Children's Prayer" from HANSEL AND GRETEL, by Humperdinck, makes good listening here.

All night, all ____ day, An-gels watch-ing o-ver me, my Lord, ____

All night, all ____ day, An-gels watch-ing o-ver me. ____

℗ Parallel listening: "Sleeping Time," from *Memories of Childhood*, Pinto. RCA Victor Basic Library.
"Lullaby," Brahms. RCA Victor Basic Library.
"Cradle Song," Schubert. RCA Victor Basic Library.

Schlaf, Kindlein, Schlaf

TRANSLATED BY V. S. BURRINGTON
GERMAN FOLK SONG

It's never too early to begin learning a foreign language. Instead of "Sleep, baby, sleep," try singing these words in German. They are pronounced shlahf, kint-line, shlahf.

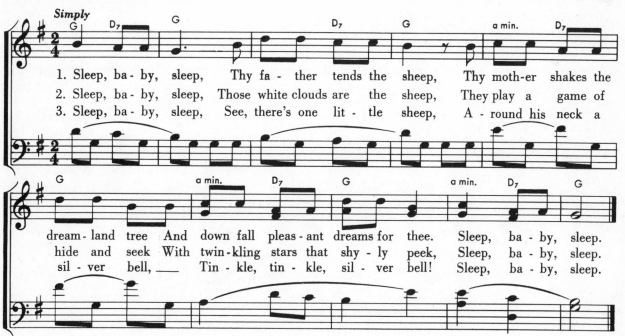

1. Sleep, ba-by, sleep, Thy fa-ther tends the sheep, Thy moth-er shakes the
2. Sleep, ba-by, sleep, Those white clouds are the sheep, They play a game of
3. Sleep, ba-by, sleep, See, there's one lit-tle sheep, A-round his neck a

dream-land tree And down fall pleas-ant dreams for thee. Sleep, ba-by, sleep.
hide and seek With twin-kling stars that shy-ly peek, Sleep, ba-by, sleep.
sil-ver bell, ____ Tin-kle, tin-kle, sil-ver bell! Sleep, ba-by, sleep.

Five Angels

TRANSLATED BY ADINA WILLIAMSON
GERMAN FOLK SONG

*After a brief period of rest, with eyes closed, it's
pleasant to be wakened with music.*

Five an-gels ring a-round my bed. "Get up," they sing,"you sleep-y-head."

The first one lights the fire, The sec-ond one but-ters the bread,
The third one pours the milk, The fourth one sets the table,

The fifth one whis-pers soft-ly, "Come, sleep-y-head, hop out of bed."

Parallel listening: "Hush, My Babe," Rousseau. RCA Victor Basic Library.
Parallel listening: "Lullaby," Mozart. RCA Victor Basic Library.

Little Hamster

WORDS AND MUSIC BY CLARA ELLEN SPELMAN

*What six-year-old hasn't sung to his pet as he
plays with him, strokes his fur, feeds him?*

1. I like your fur, I like your ti-ny size, I
2. Your wheel goes turn-ing round and round and round, And

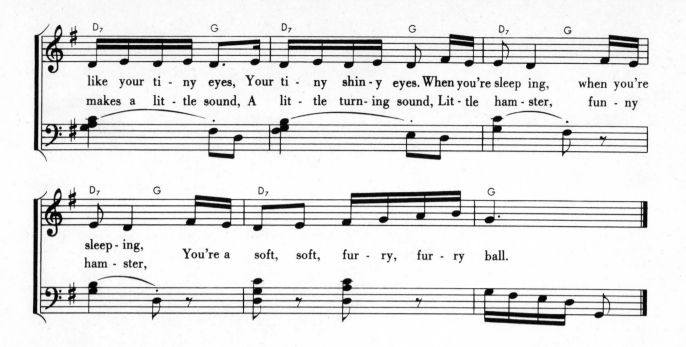

like your ti - ny eyes, Your ti - ny shin - y eyes. When you're sleep - ing, when you're
makes a lit - tle sound, A lit - tle turn - ing sound, Lit - tle ham - ster, fun - ny

sleep - ing, You're a soft, soft, fur - ry, fur - ry ball.
ham - ster,

As the children dramatize this song, adapt the accompaniment to suit the mood and movement of each verse. Play it both fast and slow, in major (as written) and in minor (ignoring the sharps), to give the music a feeling of mystery.

The Old Gray Cat

ALABAMA FOLK SONG

Moderately

1. The old gray cat is sleep - ing, sleep - ing,
2. The lit - tle mice are creep - ing, creep - ing,

sleep - ing, The old gray cat is sleep - ing in the house.
creep - ing, The lit - tle mice are creep - ing through the house.

Parallel listening: "Cat and Mouse," Copland. Decca.

3. The little mice are nibbling in the house.
4. The little mice are sleeping in the house.
5. The old gray cat comes creeping through the house.
6. The little mice all scamper through the house.

The game begins with the cat (one child) lying on the floor with eyes closed. As the mice scamper through the house, the cat tries to catch a child, who becomes the cat. To prolong movement between verses, play drum:

My Little Dog

FOLK SONG FROM THE NORTH OF ENGLAND
COLLECTED BY JEAN RITCHIE

With an easy swing

Have you news of my lit-tle dog? Oh, yes, he's out in the

fields - O! He's wag-ging his tail as he jumps up and down, Woof

woof! Woof woof! He's run-ning a-long in the fields - O!

Children will find their own ways to fold up snugly on the floor, like a closed "jack-in-the-box." On the words "and out" all jump up quickly and stand straight. A good chance here for each "jack-in-the-box" to do his own little dance. After that, each folds up snugly again. Once in a while it adds to enjoyment and develops children's sense of timing if teacher sings their names and each pops out when he hears his own. Or numbers can be used just as well.

Jack-in-the-Box

WORDS AND MUSIC BY EVELYN H. HUNT

Rhythmically

Jack - in - the - box is fold - ed up, and no one knows he is there, ___ Till some - one comes and touch - es the hook, and out he pops in - to the air.

Interlude

rit.

Little Jumping Joan

NURSERY SONG

This is a good song for ball-bouncing. Or the children may pretend they have Pogo sticks. One day Barbara brought her Yo-yo. As she worked it up and down, teacher played this tune and said, "Now do you suppose you could all be Yo-yos?"

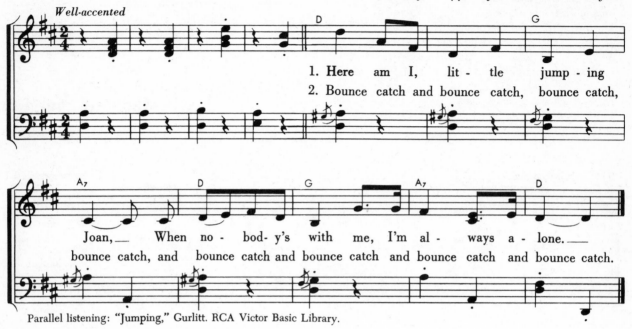

1. Here am I, lit-tle jump-ing
2. Bounce catch and bounce catch, bounce catch,

Joan,___ When no-bod-y's with me, I'm al-ways a-lone.___
bounce catch, and bounce catch and bounce catch and bounce catch and bounce catch.

Parallel listening: "Jumping," Gurlitt. RCA Victor Basic Library.

Our Clock

WORDS AND MUSIC BY MILTON KAYE

Children will want to make clock sounds with their instruments as they sing this song. Twelve children may stand in a circle, making the clock's face, while the group follows the hands around.

My friend the clock works all day long, Hap-pi-ly

tick-ing and tock-ing his song, Now let's all fol-low his

40

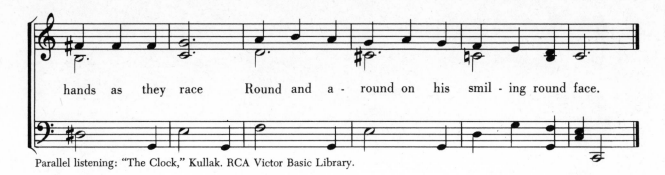

hands   as   they   race   Round   and   a - round   on   his   smil - ing   round   face.

Parallel listening: "The Clock," Kullak. RCA Victor Basic Library.

Here is another good bouncing tune which the children will enjoy in many ways. The last phrase is easy to play on glasses or melody bells.

Little Red Wagon

PLAY-PARTY GAME

1. Rid - ing   up   and   down   in   the   lit - tle   red   wag - on,
2. Hey! __   what's __   happened   to   the   lit - tle   red   wag - on?

Rid - ing   up   and   down   in   the   lit - tle   red   wag - on,   Rid - ing   up   and   down   in   the
Hey! __   what's __ happened   to   the   lit - tle   red   wag - on?   Hey! __   what's __ happened   to   the

lit - tle   red   wag - on,   Won't   you   be   my   dar - ling?
lit - tle   red   wag - on?   Won't   you   be   my   dar - ling?

3. One wheel's off and the axle's dragging. (3 times)
   Won't you be my darling?

4. Hush your mouth and stop your bragging.

5. Or you'll fall out of the little red wagon.

Some children may turn their arms to simulate wheels going around, others may pull the wagon or drive one powered by a motor.

41

In the Garden

ADAPTED FROM AN OLD SONG

Briskly

It was bright and sun - ny weath-er when we woke up to - day, ___ The

bell rang out to say, "Get up, to - day is rak - ing day." And it's

rake, rake, rake, rake, rake, rake a - way. _____ We're

all at work in the gar - den on a rak - ing day. _____

42

This woodpecker may tap on an old maple tree or the elm in your vicinity or even on a telephone pole. Of course his pecking will be echoed by wood blocks and rhythm sticks.

The Woodpecker

WORDS AND MUSIC BY ERNEST GOLD

In narrative style

With a ta-ka-ta-ka-tak and a peck-peck-peck, The wood-peck-er says hel-

lo. With a ta-ka-ta-ka-tak and a peck-peck-peck, He

works till the sun is low. He pecks a-way at the old ap-ple tree, Nev-er

once does he rest his neck. He goes ta-ka-ta-ka-ta-ka-ta-ka-

ta-ka-ta-ka-ta-ka-ta-ka-tak, peck-peck-peck-peck.

Diddle-dy Diddle-dy

WORDS ADAPTED BY KATE COX GODDARD
MUSIC BY LADY BELL

"Humpity inch worms measuring here to there, with the greatest care" are also in the garden. Perhaps lightning bugs, too. Dramatizing this song may well become a nature lesson.

1. Did - dle - dy, did - dle - dy, did - dle dy, did - dle - dy,
   Bees are buzz-ing a - mong the flowers, Did - dle - dy, did - dle - dy,
   did - dle - dy, did - dle - dy, Bees are bus - y in sun - shine and showers.

2. Wig - gle - ly, wig - gle - ly, wig - gle - ly, wig - gle - ly,
   Cat - er - pil - lars crawl up and down, Wig - gle - ly, wig - gle - ly,
   wig - gle - ly, wig - gle - ly, Cat - er - pil - lars are fuz - zy and brown.

3. Flittery, fluttery, flittery, fluttery,
   Butterflies in the sun today,
   Flittery, fluttery, flittery, fluttery,
   Butterflies spread their wings bright and gay.

4. Hippity, hoppity, hippity, hoppity,
   Toad goes hopping along the way,
   Hippity, hoppity, hippity, hoppity,
   Toad keeps snapping at flies all the day.

The Caterpillars

MARY, EL CENTRO SCHOOL
SOUTH PASADENA, CALIFORNIA

Wig - gle, wig - gle go the cat - er - pil - lars,

Wig - gle, wig - gle go the cat - er - pil - lars!

44

The Lawn Mower

WORDS BY DOROTHY BARUCH
MUSIC BY MILTON KAYE

Instead of handing out rhythm instruments, teacher talked to her children one
day about all of us having instruments "in us." After a little, they caught the
idea that stamping with our feet and clapping with our hands make "instrument" sounds. So then there was a "band," with children choosing to be "clappers," "stampers," and "singers." The "singers" then sang "The Lawn Mower"
song, while the "clappers" chanted the "Zwuzz, wisssh," and the "stampers"
acted out the role of gardener cutting the lawn.

Poem "The Lawn Mower" from I LIKE MACHINERY, published by Harper & Brothers.

The Garden Wall

ALABAMA FOLK SONG

Deliberately

1. Oh, broth - er, ___ let's go round the wall. ___
2. Oh, sis - ter, ___ let's go round the wall. ___

Don't let me lin - ger, ___ don't let me fall.
Don't let me lin - ger, ___ don't let me fall.

Tops spin gaily to this song. Or children may lie on the floor and pretend to pedal bicycles. When teacher sings "Come, Sam, let's go round the wall," Sam smiles and quickly joins the group.

Try approaching Sam with a smile and a gaily sung, "Come, Sam, let's go round the wall," some-day when he doesn't want to paint, and see how quickly he accepts your proffered hand and joins the group. Sally, who's shy, wants to come, too.

We All Need Homes

GROUP OF CHILDREN
DALTON SCHOOL, NEW YORK CITY

Squir - rels need homes, ants need homes, Birds need homes, peo - ple need homes.

I Like the Country

3

JUMP OR JIGGLE

Frogs jump
Caterpillars hump

Worms wiggle
Bugs jiggle

Rabbits hop
Horses clop

Snakes slide
Seagulls glide

Mice creep
Deer leap

Puppies bounce
Kittens pounce

Lions stalk—
But—
I walk!

—Evelyn Beyer

Music can give us the freshness and charm of life in the country. It can re-create the experiences most children have had, for real effort is being made today to give every city child some place in the sun, during vacation time. Here, then, are songs about the country for children everywhere to use and enjoy.

Details will differ in various parts of the country. Some children will be familiar with corn, others with sugar cane. Thus, many suggestions are offered for adapting a song to various locales. To be vital, songs and dramatic play must be based on real life experience.

In rhythmic action and dramatic play, for which there are such rich opportunities, try to get the feeling of wide and open space. Movements should be easy and relaxed. When different activities are adapted to a song, be sure to vary the tempo to suit each activity.

Country sounds have a character all their own. These may be studied at first hand, if possible . . . animal sounds, natural sounds of rain and tree movement in the wind, the clatter of farm chores being done, and so on. Children can gain real values by imitating these sounds with voice or with instruments.

The poetry of these songs tells of country things. Emphasize it. Singing and poetry can sometimes be used alternately. For an example of this, see "Work Horses," on p. 62.

Joe Rattle

WORDS FROM THE DUTCH
PENNSYLVANIA FOLK SONG

Even those children whose lives are circumscribed by hard city pavements "come out on the grass" with joy. Racial memory is strong. Stronger still is man's tie to, and love for, animals.

Joe Rat-tle, Joe Rat-tle, come out on the grass, Where the bird-ies keep whis-tling as the rab-bits hop past. You'll see the ox danc-ing, you'll hear the cow moo, While the mule beats a drum __ for me and for you!

Children will want to be birdies, rabbits, oxen, cows, and mules in turn. The song may be sung five times over to give enough time for the pantomiming of each animal. At first the children's own ideas of how each animal moves will be better than anything that teacher might suggest, since children move more freely when they are carrying out their own ideas. Later, suggestions may be in order. "What else do rabbits do beside hop?" "Has anyone ever watched birds to see if they sing while they fly?" "How do you suppose the mule beats a drum with his tail, when he can't see it?"

Occasionally Mary Jones, Juan Ortiz, and others like to be invited into the circle, instead of Joe Rattle. Each improvises his own dance as he comes, while Peter or Jane or all of us beat the drum "for me and for you." Because it repeats itself so often, this tune is easy to play by ear on the melody bells or the piano.

This dramatization may be a re-creation of life in the country, bringing the fragrance of fresh-cut hay to mind even though the classroom windows are banked with snow.

Let's Go Walking

SATIS N. COLEMAN AND ALICE G. THORN

Lightly

Let's go walk-ing, walk-ing, walk-ing, Let's go walk-ing far, far a-way; Let's walk back a-gain, back a-gain, back a-gain, Let's walk home a-gain, back the same day.

℞ Parallel listening: "Country Gardens" (English Folk). RCA Victor Basic Library.

Let's go walking:
> up the mountain or up in the hills,
> all through the woods,
> down by the stream (or creek),
> in the alfalfa,
> out in the meadow or pasture,
> to the cornfield (adapt to locale),
> to find wild strawberries,
> to pick sand plums,
> to the corral.

Let's go walking to many other places, too. Then let's walk back again. This helps our children to "feel" the length of a phrase—not that we'll burden them by explaining just what a phrase is.

Down in the Grain Fields

FOLK SONG FROM SCOTLAND
COLLECTED BY JEAN RITCHIE

Vigorously

1. Down in the grain - fields jig - ging it, jig - ging it,
2. Down in the grain - fields jog - ging it, jog - ging it,

Down in the grain - fields jig- ging a - long. Down in the grain - fields
Down in the grain - fields jog- ging a - long. Down in the grain - fields

50

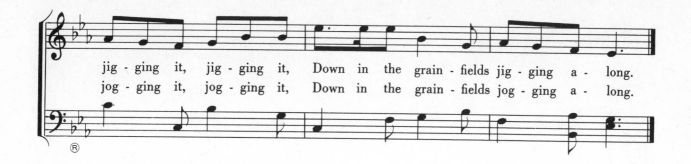

jig - ging it, jig - ging it, Down in the grain - fields jig - ging a - long.
jog - ging it, jog - ging it, Down in the grain - fields jog - ging a - long.

If all the animals on a farm say "Good day" in such a pleasant manner, a bright "Good morning" for our friends must be a nice custom for six-year-olds to follow, too.

Morning on the Farm

WORDS AND MUSIC BY LADY BELL

1. When sheep get up in the morn - ing, they al - ways say, "Good day," When
2. When cats get up in the morn - ing, they al - ways say, "Good day," When

sheep get up in the morn - ing, they al - ways say, "Good day."
cats get up in the morn - ing, they al - ways say, "Good day."

"Baa, baa, baa, baa," that is what they say, they say.
"Meow, meow, meow, meow," that is what they say, they say.

"Baa, baa, baa, baa," that is what they say.
"Meow, meow, meow, meow," that is what they say.

Five Black Horses

WORDS BY V. S. BURRINGTON
FOLK SONG FROM SCOTLAND

Children will want to make verses, to sing about things that interest them most. To add zest to the singing, try raising the pitch of this song for different verses.

One and one is two, and an-oth-er one is three, and an-oth-er one is four, and an-oth-er one is five,

1. On - ly
2. On - ly

five black hors-es trot-ting down the street.
five red tu-lips in a pret-ty row.

3. Only five big pieces of that apple pie.
4. Only five tomatoes spilling on my knee.
5. Only five potatoes making eyes at me.
6. Only five spring crickets saying, "Squeak, squeak, squeak."
7. Only five cute monkeys playing hide and seek.

Old Woman and the Pig

AMERICAN FOLK SONG

1. There was an old wom-an and she had a lit-tle pig,___ Oink, oink,
2. This lit-tle old wom-an kept the pig___ in the barn,___ Oink, oink,

52

Sawing Firewood

WORDS PARAPHRASED BY ADINA WILLIAMSON
DANISH FOLK SONG

Swaying smoothly and steadily, two of us pull the big saw to and fro across the log. Also we might sing of chopping kindling with our axes. A good chance here for making up another stanza.

Vigorously

1. Back and forth we pull the saw, Back and forth we pull the saw. When the saw-dust starts to fly, It will pile up high, high, high. We are saw-ing fire - wood, Saw - ing, saw - ing, fire - wood.

2. We are strong and might-y men, We are strong and might-y men. We can make the saw-dust fly, We can pile it high, high, high. We are saw-ing fire - wood, Saw - ing, saw - ing fire - wood.

Oats, Peas, Beans

This old circle game dramatizes the farmer's work with his crops and his celebration of the harvest.

ENGLISH SINGING GAME

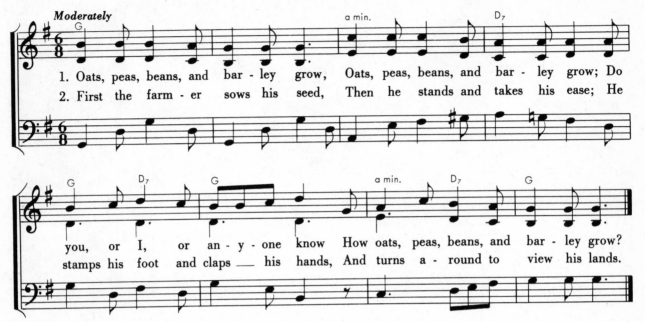

1. Oats, peas, beans, and bar - ley grow, Oats, peas, beans, and bar - ley grow; Do
2. First the farm - er sows his seed, Then he stands and takes his ease; He

you, or I, or an - y - one know How oats, peas, beans, and bar - ley grow?
stamps his foot and claps __ his hands, And turns a - round to view his lands.

3. Waiting for a partner,
   Waiting for a partner,
   Open the ring and take her in,
   While we gaily dance and sing.

My Apple Tree

If we want apples just to eat, we may shake the tree till some fall off on the ground. But with fancy apples for sale, we must climb a ladder, pick each apple carefully, and put it in a bag or basket.

WORDS PARAPHRASED BY LOUISE KESSLER
CZECH FOLK SONG

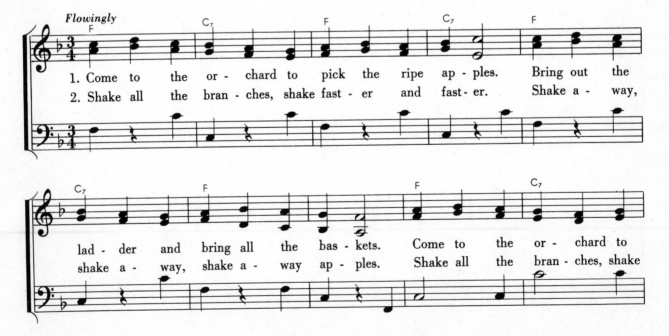

1. Come to the or - chard to pick the ripe ap - ples. Bring out the
2. Shake all the bran - ches, shake fast - er and fast - er. Shake a - way,

lad - der and bring all the bas - kets. Come to the or - chard to
shake a - way, shake a - way ap - ples. Shake all the bran - ches, shake

Going to Pasture

HEBRIDES FOLK TUNE
COLLECTED BY JEAN RITCHIE

When the cows leave the barn for pasture, they stroll along with a slow, easy rhythm. Other farm rhythms go well with this tune—pitching hay, pumping water, loading the truck, shucking corn.

Rhythmically with marked accent

® Parallel listening: "Sheep and Goats Walking to Pasture," Guion.

I See the Moon

WORDS ADAPTED
IRISH FOLK SONG

*"I see the sun . . the stars . . the clouds." These
are other beautiful things to sing about quietly.*

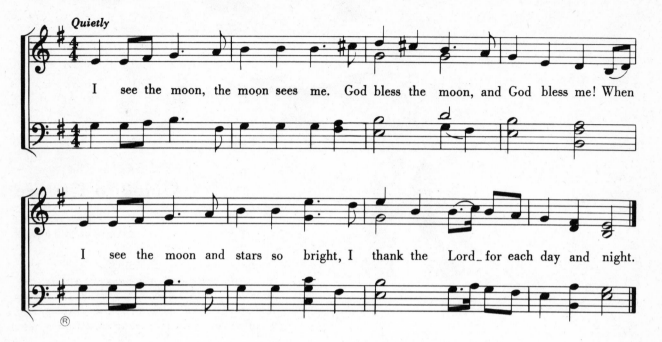

I see the moon, the moon sees me. God bless the moon, and God bless me! When

I see the moon and stars so bright, I thank the Lord for each day and night.

White Pony

WORDS BY MARION H. WALKER
MUSIC BY FLORENCE WHITE

*"My little white pony comes galloping home." Pony
and children are tired, after a good gallop. By
playing this song slowly or using a signature of
four flats, instead of one, making it minor, we can
help the children "be" tired ponies.*

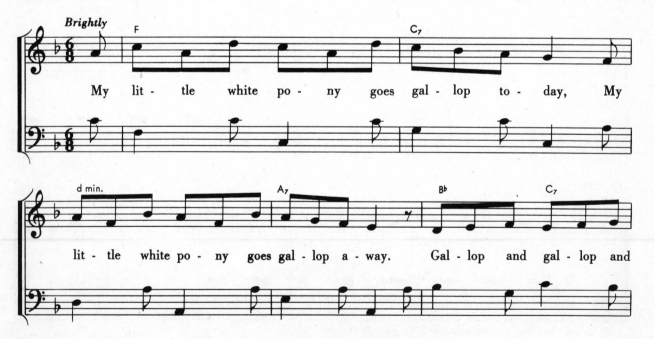

My lit - tle white po - ny goes gal - lop to - day, My

lit - tle white po - ny goes gal - lop a - way. Gal - lop and gal - lop and

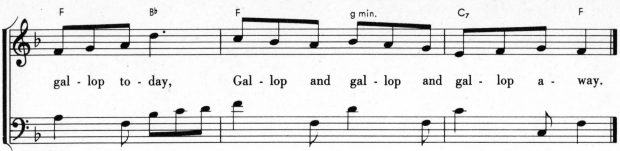

gal - lop to - day, Gal - lop and gal - lop and gal - lop a - way.

Parallel listening:
"Hobby Horse," from *Memories of Childhood,* Pinto. RCA Victor Basic Library.
"Wild Horseman," Schumann. RCA Victor Basic Library.
"Little Gray Ponies." Children's Record Guild.

And So We Ride

WORDS ADAPTED
DUTCH FOLK SONG

1. Oh, I trot trot on the bare back of a don - key, of a don - key, Oh, I

trot trot on the bare back of a don - key, with - out reins.

2. Oh, I gal - lop on a don - key, on the bare back of a don - key, Oh, I

gal - lop on a don - key, on his bare back with - out reins.

Parallel listening: "Who Wants a Ride?" Young People's Records.

Hayride

This song almost sings itself as we hitch the horses to the big hay wagon, drive the team, climb in over the big wheels, sit on the back of the wagon, dangle our feet over the edge, and tumble in the sweet-smelling hay.

WORDS BY MARION ABESON
MUSIC BY CHARITY BAILEY

Easily

1. Got my-self two hor - ses, Got my-self a wag - on,
2. If you're not too bus - y, Come a - long, get diz - zy,

Now we'll fill it full of hay - O; Then I hitch my hor - ses,
Tum - bling on a load of hay - O. Driv - ing two big hor - ses,

See Young People's Record 806, "Who Wants a Ride."

66

Jump up on the wag - on, Take the reins and drive a - way - O.
Sit - ting on a wag - on, Rid - ing on a load of hay - O.

Refrain

This way you tum - ble, That way you tum - ble, Up on a load of hay - O.

This way you tum - ble, That way you tum - ble, Up on a load of hay - O.

Skip to My Lou

AMERICAN SINGING GAME

The wholehearted nonsense of this song frees children in making similarly silly verses. "What animal shall we sing about? Where shall he be? What does he say?" With such questions, we easily get, "Cow in the pasture, moo, moo, moo."

1. Flies in the butter-milk, shoo, fly, shoo! Flies in the butter-milk, shoo, fly, shoo!
2. Little red wag-on, paint-ed blue, Little red wag-on, paint-ed blue,

Flies in the butter-milk, shoo, fly, shoo! Skip to my Lou, my dar-ling.
Little red wag-on, paint-ed blue, Skip to my Lou, my dar-ling.

Can't find my crayons, Boo, hoo, hoo (etc.)

I'll have some milk and crackers, too (etc.)

Turtle

WORDS BY JAMES TIPPETT
MUSIC BY ARTHUR EDWARDS

Some of the children will be turtles that trick-track slowly (but without stopping) over the floor. Others will enjoy hopping about the room like frogs.

1. I have not heard a tur-tle talk, Or e-ven make a
2. I have not felt a tur-tle bite, Or seen it snap its

sound,_____ But I have watched a tur-tle walk,
jaws,_____ But I have fol-lowed trick-track trails,

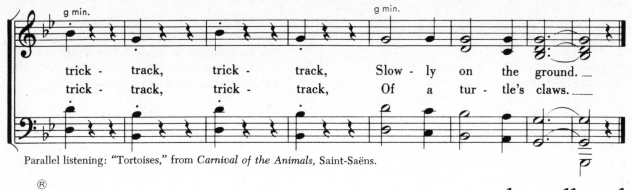

trick - track, trick - track, Slow - ly on the ground. __
trick - track, trick - track, Of a tur - tle's claws. __

Parallel listening: "Tortoises," from *Carnival of the Animals,* Saint-Saëns.

Frog in the Millpond

ALABAMA FOLK SONG

Frog in the mill - pond and can't get out, Take a lit - tle stick and

stir him all a - bout. { 1. Poke him out, poke him out, poke him out, out!
{ 2. See him hop, see him hop, see him hop out!

Frog - gie! __ frog - gie! __ frog - gie! __
Frog - gie! __ frog - gie! __ frog - gie! __

Children stand in circle to simulate millpond. The "frog," with eyes closed, squats in middle as children sing song. Children pretend to stir up frog with stick, and frog hops, in accordance with words of the song. At the end of the second verse the children continue singing "Froggie!" and the game begins. The players dare not run, they are poison if they stand, but are safe when they squat. The frog may run. He must touch someone in the circle who does not squat soon enough or who tantalizes the frog by alternating positions. The first child caught becomes frog.

The Rabbit

WORDS BY LOUISE KESSLER
FOLK SONG FROM SOUTHERN UNITED STATES

"Will you hippety-hop with me?" Children may sing an invitation to lunch, to the playground, or to a dramatization of this song. Teacher, too, uses this invitation, since it's readily accepted.

Moderately

1. Bun-ny hid-ing in the grass, Will you hip-pe-ty-hop with
2. Oh, how hun-gry you must be! Do you nib-ble the grass all

me? Bun-ny hid-ing in the grass, Will you hip-pe-ty-hop with
day? Oh, how hun-gry you must be! Do you nib-ble the grass all

me? _____ Oh, where are you hop-ping now? _____ I'm hip-pe-ty-hop-ping,
day? _____ You nib-ble my gar-den green, _____ You nib-ble and then you

too. _____ Oh, where are you hop-ping now? _____ I'll hop a-long with you.
hop! _____ You nib-ble my gar-den green, _____ And nev-er, nev-er stop.

Parallel listening: "Kangaroo," from *Carnival of the Animals*, Saint-Saëns.

70

Ways of Going Places

4

Journeys, excursions, trips . . . here is music that brings all these fascinating things to the minds of children and suggests new thoughts and feelings, too. These songs offer opportunities for larger-scale dramatizations. Every train has lots of cars, a harbor needs many kinds of boats. Whistles must blow! Here is a chance for many sound effects and for dynamic change, too, as trains approach, stop, and rush far away.

ROADWAYS

People are always moving
On foot, on horses,
On wheels, on rails,
In ships on the sea,
Now, on wings in the sky.

—LUCY SPRAGUE MITCHELL

We Go Traveling

WORDS BY W. S. WILLIAMS
FRENCH FOLK SONG

There are many places to go and many ways of getting there. The children will always enjoy the places and ways they know the best.

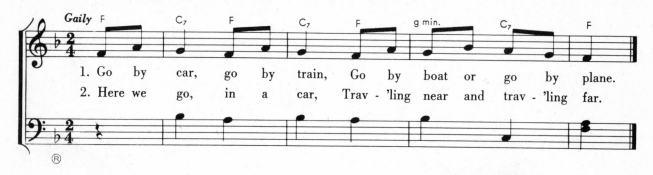

1. Go by car, go by train, Go by boat or go by plane.
2. Here we go, in a car, Trav - 'ling near and trav - 'ling far.

3. When we sail in a boat,
   On the water we will float.

4. We can ride in a train,
   In the sun and in the rain.

5. Roller skates on our feet,
   Send us rolling down the street.

6. On our bikes we will roam,
   Round the block and back to home.

7. We will ride in a bus,
   Come and wave good-bye to us.

8. In a plane we will fly,
   Soaring up into the sky.

9. We may go, very soon,
   In a space ship to the moon.

The Helicopter

GROUP OF CHILDREN, ONEONTA SCHOOL
SOUTH PASADENA, CALIFORNIA

Now that helicopters have become part of the regular mail service in many big cities, the children are used to seeing these huge birds in the sky. Some indeed call them "whirly-birds."

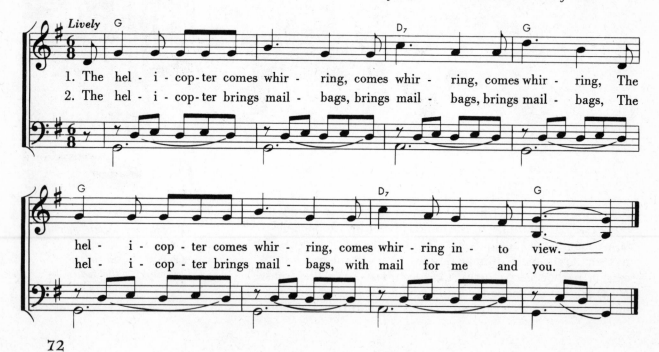

1. The hel - i - cop-ter comes whir - ring, comes whir - ring, comes whir - ring, The
2. The hel - i - cop-ter brings mail - bags, brings mail - bags, brings mail - bags, The

hel - i - cop-ter comes whir - ring, comes whir - ring in - to view. _____
hel - i - cop-ter brings mail - bags, with mail for me and you. _____

Now Let Me Fly

SPIRITUAL

"Me" in the chorus might be a bird, a kite, a jet,
an airliner, each dramatized in turn. After the song
a few might try piano improvising; some low tones,
for airplane taxiing, glissando up and down for
takeoff and descent, etc.

Way down yon-der in the mid-dle of the field, See me work-ing at the char-iot wheel. Not so par-tic-'lar 'bout work-ing at the wheel, But I just want to see how the char-iot feels. Now let me fly, _____ Now let me fly, _____ Now let me fly _____ way up high, _____ Way in the mid-dle of the air.

® Parallel listening: "Impromptu," from *Petite Suite*, Bizet. RCA Victor Basic Library.

When the Train Comes Along

AMERICAN FOLK SONG

Children like to line up behind each other and play train. Of course, the train goes fast and slow, goes through tunnels and around curves, and finally pulls into the station.

When the train comes a-long,— when the train comes a-long,— I'll

meet you at the sta-tion when the train comes a-long.

1. It may be snow-ing, It
2. It may be rain-ing, It

may be cold, But I'll meet you at the sta-tion when the train comes a-long.

may be hot, But I'll meet you at the sta-tion when the train comes a-long.

Parallel listening: "Run, Run, Run," from *Memories of Childhood*, Pinto. RCA Victor Basic Library.

Train Song

CHILDREN'S PLAY CHANT
LOS ANGELES, CALIFORNIA

Children love making up train calls, often using their favorite interval, so-mi (5-3) to chant "All aboard for Memphis!" "Train No. 2 ready on Track 4, all aboard!" etc. Good fun and good tonal play combined.

All a-board!— All a-board!— Watch out at the rail-road cross-ing.—

All a-board!— All a-board!— Beep, beep, beep, beep!

As the train gets underway, there will be shuffling steps to indicate it is gathering speed. It will pull up short when stopping for signals and ease gently into the next station.

Pufferbillies

WORDS AND MUSIC TRADITIONAL

Down at the sta - tion, ear - ly in the morn - ing, See the lit - tle

puf - fer - bil - lies lined up in a row. See the en - gine dri - ver

pull the lit - tle throt - tle. Chug! Chug! Poof! Poof! Off we go.

Ballad of the Train

JACKIE, THOMAS METCALF SCHOOL
NORMAL, ILLINOIS

Most children are vitally interested in airplanes and know the names of many of them. This song may be used as an airport song, as well as a train song, and used to call off names of planes.

Chug, chug, chug, chug, chug, chug, chug; The en - gine, the tend - er, the coal car, the oil car, the cat - tle car, the box car, the flat car, and the ca - boose. Toot, toot, here comes the train!

Toot, toot, here comes the train! Chug, chug, chug, chug, chug, chug, s - s - s - h!

All the different cars, represented by children, assemble to make up a train, as they are mentioned in the song.

Instruments can give us some good sound effects:
Sand blocks or claves clapped together will give the sound of a train being coupled together.
Slide sand blocks together to indicate gathering speed.
Slide halves of coconut shells together briskly for click of rails.
Select two low-pitched black keys on piano and play slowly, then faster, to indicate gathering speed.

Busy Switching Engine

MARY ALICE, THOMAS METCALF SCHOOL
NORMAL, ILLINOIS

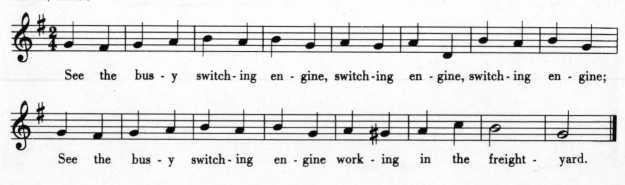

See the bus - y switch - ing en - gine, switch - ing en - gine, switch - ing en - gine; See the bus - y switch - ing en - gine work - ing in the freight - yard.

76

*Everyone will want to take turns being the Little
Red Caboose. The role may be used to help the
shy child feel important or to reward some child
for a job well done.*

Little Red Caboose

WORDS AND MUSIC BY DEKE MOFFITT

Parallel listening: "Running Horses," Anderson. RCA Victor Basic Library.

Sometimes the train comprised of children will be "coming down the track."
Starting softly, as the train is far away, the song is sung three times and made
to sound as if the train is coming nearer and nearer. Or the train may be "going
down the track," and the singing get softer and softer. It's fun to pause at the
end of the third repeat and sing *"Woo - woo"* as the "engineer" pulls the lever.

Car Song

WORDS AND MUSIC BY WOODY GUTHRIE

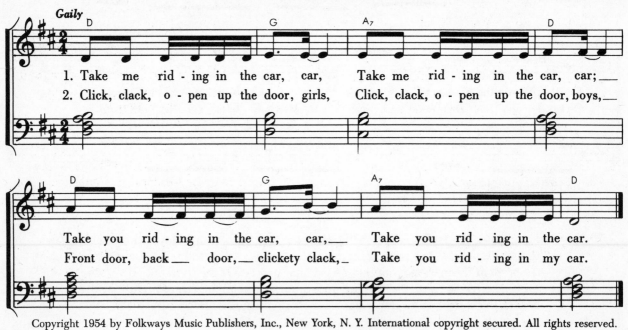

Gaily

1. Take me rid - ing in the car, car, Take me rid - ing in the car, car;__ Take you rid - ing in the car, car,__ Take you rid - ing in the car.

2. Click, clack, o - pen up the door, girls, Click, clack, o - pen up the door, boys,__ Front door, back__ door,__ clickety clack,__ Take you rid - ing in my car.

What a bewildering array of delightful things to do as we ride in our car. No day and no verse will be long enough! To extend the action, the tune may be resung to "Brrr" between verses.

3. Climb, climb around the front seat,
   Spree, I spraddle on the back seat;
   Turn my key, step on the starter,
   Take you riding in my car.

4. The engine it goes Brrr, Brrr,
   The engine it goes Brrr, Brrr;
   Front seat, back seat, boys and girls,
   Take you riding in my car.

5. Trees and houses walk along,
   Great big buildings walk along;
   Truck and car and a garbage can,
   Take you riding in my car.

Used by permission. See also Folkways Record FP 5.

6. Well, ships and little boats chug along,
   Ships and little boats chug along;
   Brrr, Brrr, Brrr, Brrr,
   Take you riding in my car.

7. I'm going to zoom you home again,
   I'm going to zoom you home again;
   Brrr, Brrr, roll-y home,
   Take you riding in my car.

8. I'm going to let you blow the horn,
   I'm going to let you blow the horn;
   Rrrrr, Rrrrr, Rrrrr, Rrrrr,
   Take you riding in my car.

Bell Buoys

GROUP OF CHILDREN
NEW YORK CITY SCHOOL

*The bell buoys anchored in the harbor are buf-
feted by wind and wave. "Come, let's be bell
buoys and sway to and fro." Sand blocks may be
used for the swaying and triangles for the ringing.*

1. Bell buoys are sway - ing, Bell buoys are sway - ing,
2. Bell buoys are ring - ing, Bell buoys are ring - ing,

See how the light shines a - bove. _____
Hear how the bells sing a tune. _____

Look out! __ Look out __ for rocks and for bro - ken boats. ____

There is variance in both meter and key in these songs made up by children
and recorded exactly as they were sung. Children, when young and free, do
not bother about the conventions; they are unaware of them. It is better to
keep their fresh viewpoint than to pour children's ideas into a mold.

Rolling Along

FRENCH-CANADIAN SONG

*This little bit, from a French voyageur song, is
good for paddling imaginary canoes. It may also
be used for ball-rolling; try rolling a ball so that
it stops at the end of the song.*

Roll - ing, roll - ing, roll - ing a - long, See my ball a - roll - ing on.

As we sing we may be riding in a sailboat with hands on the tiller. Or we may even be the high wind-filled sails of the sailboat itself or a sharp prow cutting through the water.

The Sailboat Song

WORDS AND MUSIC BY ERNEST GOLD

Sail a - long, sail a - long! The wa - ter is smooth, and the

breeze is strong. White are your sails, and tall stands the mast; The

spray wets my face, we're mov - ing so fast. Sail a - long,

sail a - long! The o - cean is wide, and the jour - ney is long!

Sail a - long, sail a - long!

Parallel listening: "Barcarolle," from *Tales of Hoffman*, Offenbach.

Little Tugboat

GROUP OF CHILDREN
NEW YORK CITY SCHOOL

The children who play the role of tugboat must get the steamboat safely into its berth. It takes much gentle nudging to turn a big ship around. Or they can push or pull barges up and down the river.

Oh, the stump-y lit-tle tug-boat, Works in the riv-er, Pull-ing barg-es up and down, up and down.

The Big Steamer

GROUP OF CHILDREN
NEW YORK CITY SCHOOL

Amid all the fun of blowing out great clouds of smoke and "Too-tooing," all the steamboats must remember that they are carrying human lives and precious cargo safely across the sea.

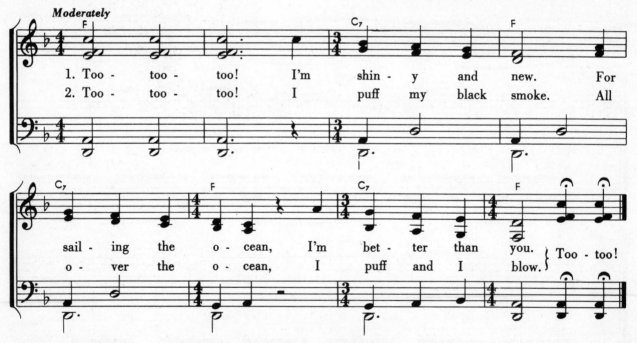

1. Too - too - too! I'm shin-y and new. For sail-ing the o-cean, I'm bet-ter than you. { Too - too!
2. Too - too - too! I puff my black smoke. All o-ver the o-cean, I puff and I blow. }

3. Too-too-too! I blow my foghorn.
   When fog's on the ocean, I send my alarm.

82

Ferry boats carry people across rivers or other waterways. Ferries load cars, too, on the lower deck. Men are needed to collect the money, to keep the cars in line, and tell them when to go.

Ferry Boats

4-YEAR-OLD CHILD
LITCHFIELD, CONNECTICUT

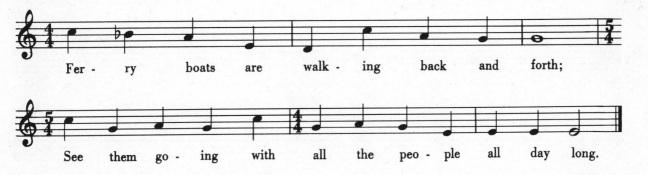

Fer - ry boats are walk - ing back and forth;

See them go - ing with all the peo - ple all day long.

The Gallant Ship

ENGLISH FOLK SONG
COLLECTED AND ARRANGED BY CECIL J. SHARP

A round and round song for many purposes. Matching action to the phrase lengths of this song is easier with smaller circles, which have time to go round three times before sinking into the sea.

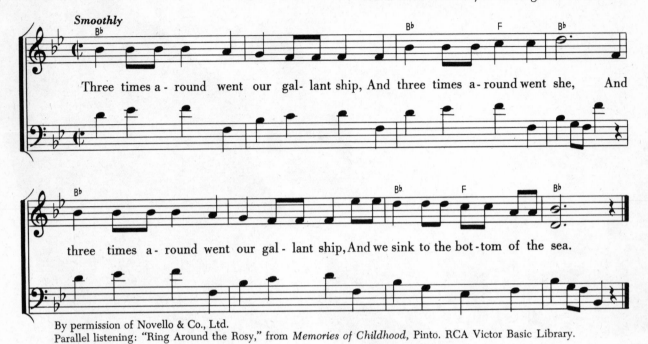

Three times a-round went our gal-lant ship, And three times a-round went she, And

three times a-round went our gal-lant ship, And we sink to the bot-tom of the sea.

By permission of Novello & Co., Ltd.
Parallel listening: "Ring Around the Rosy," from *Memories of Childhood*, Pinto. RCA Victor Basic Library.

Up She Rises

SEA CHANTEY

Good sailors heave up the anchor, hoist sails, and do many other chores while they sing. And when Dick falls down and skins a knee, tears can be easily dried with "Aye, aye, and up he rises."

Aye, aye, and up she ris-es, Aye, aye, and up she ris-es;

Aye, aye, and up she ris-es, We're off a-cross the o-cean.

It's a proud thing to be a lighthouse, with the responsibility of guiding safely to harbor all of the children playing the role of boats.

The Lighthouse

GROUP OF CHILDREN
NEW YORK CITY SCHOOL

I'd like to be a light-house, a-stand-ing by the sea. I'd turn my light for all the boats that passed by me.

Parallel listening: "What the Lighthouse Sees." Young People's Records.
"Flying Birds," Anderson. RCA Victor Basic Library.

How many interesting things go on in the harbor and how enjoyably they can be dramatized! Waves come rolling in; sea gulls glide and swoop; bell buoys clang rhythmically; a lighthouse stands straight and tall, flashing at intervals; a big steamer comes slowly in, blowing its whistle and passing ferry boats crowded with people. Tugs chug out to meet it and nudge it into dock; and then the unloading starts, with cranes hard at work.

Row, Row, Row Your Boat

TRADITIONAL

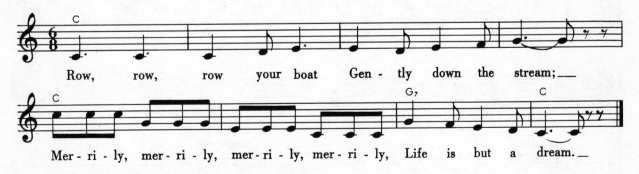

Row, row, row your boat Gen-tly down the stream;— Mer-ri-ly, mer-ri-ly, mer-ri-ly, mer-ri-ly, Life is but a dream.—

Parallel listening: "Boating on the Lake," Kullak. RCA Victor Basic Library.

The Pounding Waves

WORDS ADAPTED FROM POEM BY DOROTHY ALDIS
MUSIC BY ERNEST GOLD

The pound - ing waves a - long the shore Chase each oth - er with a roar. They raise their heads, and wide and high Toss their hair a - gainst the sky._____ They're white and froth - y, reach - ing tall; With a roar they break _____ and fall._____

I Like the City

5

I love the city, I find many things to do,
I play in the park, I go to the zoo.
In my apartment I have toys and games,
And so many picture books
I can't tell their names.
I stand at my window, I see a whole fleet
Of streetcars and taxis and trucks in the street.

—JAMES S. TIPPETT

The city as well as the country is full of interest for every child. All kinds of city situations may be dramatized, with attention focussed on environmental sounds. City sounds are distinctive. Children listen to them, discuss them, and imitate with voice or instrument. The range is from soft to very loud.

Here is a chance to develop an awareness of dynamics, too. Children should also be encouraged to listen for street cries and to invent some of their own. Since city children must pay attention to how they move about, here is the place to introduce moving on a set signal, as in "Stop-Go" and "Statue Game."

Bus Song

WORDS AND MUSIC BY HELEN CHRISTIANSON

Buses carry people about the city and through the country; they carry children to and from school. Your children will want to sing about the kind and color of bus that they know best.

1. We're go-ing for a ride. We're go-ing for a ride. We're go-ing for a ride in a big green bus. Will you come a-long? Will you come a-long? Will you come a-long and have a ride with us?

2. Yes, I'll come a-long. Yes, I'll come a-long. Yes, I'll come a-long for a ride with you. Driv-er, stop the bus. Driv-er, stop the bus. We're go-ing for a ride a-long the av-e-nue.

This song can be kept fresh and new by adding countless verses. The verses you will want to add will depend on the type of bus your children ride. Here are a few suggestions:

> *Wheels go round and round on the big green bus*
> *Windshield wipers click on the big green bus*
> *Put your money into the money box*
> *We're bouncing up and down over bumpy streets*
> *Now we're riding smooth, down the avenue*
> *Better ring the bell, for I get off next*
> *Turn the headlights on, for it's getting dark*
> *Standing room is left, better hold on tight*

When the song is dramatized, there is something for everyone to do. Every bus needs passengers and a driver, of course. Children learn how to be fair about taking turns as they exchange this important role. Besides, it is fun to be a windshield wiper or a big headlight that remembers to dim as another bus approaches. There will need to be wheels, too, that turn round and round.

88

Busy Trucks

WORDS AND MUSIC BY EVA A. SANDERSON

A big truck starting slowly sings low. As it goes faster, it sings higher and higher. Low-high tones on piano will tell the story. Tone blocks, sand blocks, drums, help to dramatize various trucks.

Sand trucks, grav-el trucks, big old ce-ment trucks, Build me a road, a road to the sea; So I can ride a-long, ride a-long, ride a-long, And jump in-to the o-cean, one, two, three! Whee!

The Drill

GROUP OF CHILDREN
DALTON SCHOOL, NEW YORK CITY

Six-year-olds on a field trip watched road repair work. Back in their classroom each chose a spot on the floor to "drill," and this song emerged as part of the "telling process." They sang, too, about dump trucks and cement mixers.

Brr - rr! Brr - rr! We tear up the street, Brr - rr! Brr - rr! We break through the con - crete.

89

Big Machines

WORDS AND MUSIC BY N. VACIO

A cymbal played with a soft beater will catch the swing of the crane, while large sand blocks huff and puff for bull-dozers.

Ponderously

1. Cree - ee - k! Cree - ee - k!
2. Pu - uu - sh! Pu - uu - sh!

That's the way it starts to work.
That's the way it starts to work.

Cree - ee - k! Cree - ee - k!
Pu - uu - sh! Pu - uu - sh!

Down it comes to pick up its load;
Huff - ing, puff - ing, push-es the dirt;

Big claws, big claws, My big crane.
Big bull - doz - er Huffs and puffs.

Swing down—dig—pull up—swing around and up—dump. The clumsy, ponderous rhythm of the steam shovel is easily caught. We'll need different instruments to accompany the digging and dumping and, afterward, the clanking away.

The Steam Shovel

WORDS AND MUSIC BY MILTON KAYE

What does a steam shov-el do all day? It digs, it dumps. And swings a-round like a clum-sy bear, With its load of earth from an-y-where. What does a steam shov-el do all day? It digs, it dumps, It digs, it dumps. And nois-i-ly clanks a-way, a-way, And nois-i-ly clanks a-way.

Playing Fireman

WORDS BY ELEANOR GRAHAM VANCE
MUSIC BY MARION BAUER

The wail of the siren, rising and falling, sounds far down the street. The "bong bong" of the bell clears the way. The firemen jump off, raise the ladder, unwind the hose, and are putting out the fire almost before the truck has stopped.

Bong! Bong! Bong! Bong! Where's the fire? Where's the fire? Bong! Bong! Bong! Bong!

Start the truck! Start the truck! Bong! Bong! Bong! Bong! Squirt the hose! Squirt the hose!

Bong! Bong! Bong! Bong! Put the fire out! Put the fire out!

Everyone clamors for a turn at being policeman, while the others are trucks, cars, or pedestrians.

Stop-Go

WORDS BY DOROTHY BARUCH
MUSIC BY ARTHUR EDWARDS

All of the cars In a row Wait to go While the sig-nal says: STOP.

Bells ring Ting-a-ling! Red light's gone! Green light's on! Horns blow!

And the row ___ Starts to GO.

I Am a Jolly Sweeper

GROUP OF CHILDREN
DALTON SCHOOL, NEW YORK CITY

It's fun to be anyone in uniform. It's handy for teacher to have a crew of sweepers ready for action when emergencies arise.

I'm a jol-ly sweep-er that sweeps all day, I sweep up glass and pa-per a-way. I sweep and I sweep, and I'm ver-y gay, And now I throw it all a-way.

Hat Man

CINCINNATI SCHOOL CHILDREN

As for buying and selling, that's so much a part of real life children are always in practice for playing such a role.

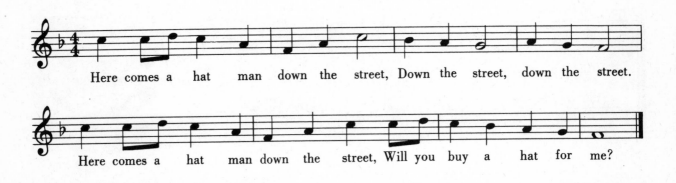

Here comes a hat man down the street, Down the street, down the street. Here comes a hat man down the street, Will you buy a hat for me?

Going to the Lumberyard

ALABAMA FOLK SONG

I'm going to the old brickyard . . to the city park. This is a song that whets the appetite for an actual trip into the community . . for an imaginary journey . . for going anywhere one wants to go (or doesn't, teachers please note).

Liltingly

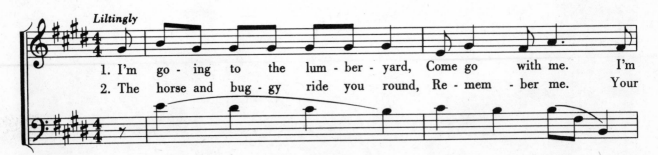

1. I'm go-ing to the lum-ber-yard, Come go with me. I'm
2. The horse and bug-gy ride you round, Re-mem-ber me. Your

94

go - ing to the lum - ber - yard, Come go with me.
lit - tle foot shan't touch the ground, Re - mem - ber me.

*It's fascinating to watch the shoemaker at his work.
We can then try to do the job ourselves. Rhythm
sticks make a good "rack-a-tack" sound.*

The Shoemaker

WORDS ANONYMOUS
MUSIC BY MILTON KAYE

Moderately

1. As I was a - walk - ing the oth - er day, I
2. With a bright lit - tle awl___ he makes a hole

passed by a win - dow just o - ver the way, And there in - side, al - most
Right through the up - per and then through the sole. He puts in a peg, then he

hid - den from view, I saw a shoe - mak - er a - mak - ing a shoe.
puts___ in two, And a ha - ha - ha - ha, and he ham - mers it through.

Refrain

With a rack-a - tack - tack and a rack-a - tack - too, This is the way he makes a shoe.

95

Street Cries

FROM NEW YORK

New po - ta - toes; red, ripe to - ma - toes!

1. Any locks to fix, ___ or keys to make? ___
2. Um - brellas to mend, ___ or knives to grind? ___

1. "Eve - ning pa - pers! Five cents a cop - y."
2. "Here comes the icecream man! Ten cents for ice-cream."
3. "Here comes the flower man! Ros - es and tu - lips."

1. Mar - y had a lit - tle lamb, lit - tle lamb, lit - tle lamb,
2. Mer - ri - ly we roll a - long, roll a - long, roll a - long,

Mar - y had a lit - tle lamb; Its fleece was white as snow.
Mer - ri - ly we roll a - long, ___ On the deep blue sea.

96

Do you know the grocery man, the garbage man, the banker, the bus driver, the ice cream man, the carpenter, the traffic cop? Or make this song a guessing game; child dramatizes and sings, "Oh, do you know who I am?"

Do You Know?

SINGING GAME

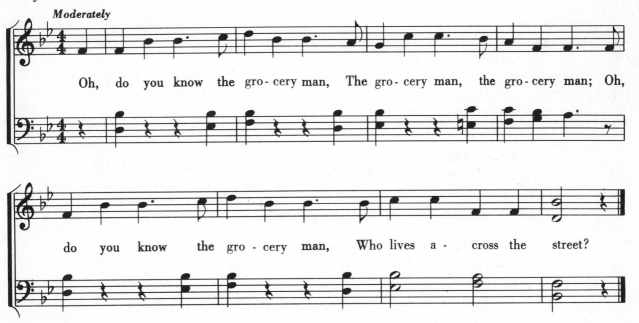

Oh, do you know the gro-cery man, The gro-cery man, the gro-cery man; Oh, do you know the gro-cery man, Who lives a-cross the street?

Like Me

WORDS BY DOROTHY ALDIS
MUSIC BY ERNEST GOLD

How many things that are important to us are done by different men! The garbage man, the policeman, the mailman, and many others.

A gar-bage man is a gar-bage man Who rat-tles and bangs the gar-bage can.

Like me. A po-lice-man car-ries a stick in his hand.

Like me. The mail-man car-ries a bag. Like mine. And they

all of them al-ways have a good time. Like me.

This song simply asks for dramatization and also for colorful and humorous sound effects. Some sound effects are written into the accompaniment, but the children will enjoy choosing many of their own. What shall we use for the rattling of garbage cans? Triangles, cymbals, or something else? For the bang of the policeman's stick? Tone blocks, perhaps? What instrument do we have that sounds like the ice cream man's bells?

Children form a ring. The child in the center makes various motions which the others imitate as they sing. He may stand on one foot, kneel, bounce a ball, pretend to be a policeman, etc.

Watch That Lady

CHILDREN'S STREET GAME
COLLECTED BY HAROLD COURLANDER

This is an old street game. Often, in street games, words seem unintelligible and yet they sing well. Originally "key" probably had some meaning in the game which, during long usage, has been lost. Many songs come down to us with words meant for the ear rather than the intellect. If we furrow our brows trying to be literal about them, all we do is spoil the fun.

See Folkways Record FP 704, "Ring Games."

Hurdy-Gurdy

WORDS BY ELEANOR FARJEON
MUSIC BY ERNEST GOLD

Joyously, but not too fast

1. Can you dance? I love to dance! Mu-sic is my hap-py chance. Mu-sic play-ing in the street
2. Can you sing? I love to sing! Mu-sic, like a bird in spring, With a gold and sil-ver note,

Gets in-to my hands and feet.
Gets in-to my heart and throat.

3. Can you play?
   I'd love to play!
Play some music every day
   Then you'll give
   The world a chance
   To dance and sing,
   To sing and dance.

Parallel listening: "Hurdy-Gurdy Man," from *Kaleidoscope*, Goossens. RCA Victor Basic Library.

This is a counting song. As children dramatize it a concept of numbers materializes, laying a foundation for addition and subtraction. There is nice contrast between glad and sad mood, too.

Three Blue Pigeons

AMERICAN FOLK SONG

1. Three blue pi - geons sit - ting on the wall.
2. Two blue pi - geons sit - ting on the wall.

Three blue pi - geons _ sit - ting on the wall. **(Words in italics are to be spoken after verse.)**
Two blue pi - geons _ sit - ting on the wall.

1. *One flew away.*
   O-o-oh!

2. *Another flew away.*
   O-o-o-o-oh!

3. One blue pigeon sitting on the wall.
   One blue pigeon sitting on the wall.

   And the third flew away!
   O-o-o-o-o-o-oh!

4. No blue pigeons sitting on the wall.
   No blue pigeons sitting on the wall.

   One flew back.
   Whee-ee-ee!

5. One blue pigeon sitting on the wall.
   One blue pigeon sitting on the wall.

   Another flew back.
   Whee-ee-ee-ee!

6. Two blue pigeons sitting on the wall.
   Two blue pigeons sitting on the wall.

   And the third flew back!
   Whee-ee-ee-ee-ee-ee!

7. Three blue pigeons sitting on the wall.
   Three blue pigeons sitting on the wall.
   (Jubilantly)

101

Jigglity-Jogglety

WORDS BY EMILIE POULSSON
MUSIC BY ERNEST GOLD

Sometimes instead of playing on the sidewalk in front of our house, we go jiggling away to a park or neighborhood playground to play.

Jig - gli - ty - jog - gle - ty shakes my load,

As I go trudg - ing a - long the road. Jig - gli - ty - jog - gle - ty,

flip - pi - ty - flop, Wib - bli - ty - wob - ble - ty till I stop.

Swinging High

WORDS AND MUSIC BY DONALD SHERRARD

Who hasn't sung to himself as he swings higher and higher and then relaxes "to let the old cat die?" It's fun to swing and sing in school, too, even though we only pretend to swing. Finger cymbals and triangle make a good accompaniment.

Swing - ing high, to the sky, Just like the birds that fly,___

Mer - ri - ly swing - ing, all the time sing - ing, Oh, what a won - der - ful time! ___

Sliding

When children are encouraged to play "Down the
slide we ride," and "Down we come again," on
melody bells, they can see as well as hear that the
tune moves down.

WORDS BY MARCETTE CHUTE
MUSIC BY ERNEST GOLD

Down the slide we ride, we ride. Round we run, and then,

Up we pop to reach the top, Down we come a - gain.

The Seesaw

The very best seesaws to rock up and down with
this song are made by pairs of children, facing,
with joined hands and outstretched arms. Pitches
go up and down, too. This song may be used for
a pitch game. See alternate pitches, last measure.

WORDS BY EVELYN BEYER
MUSIC BY ARTHUR EDWARDS

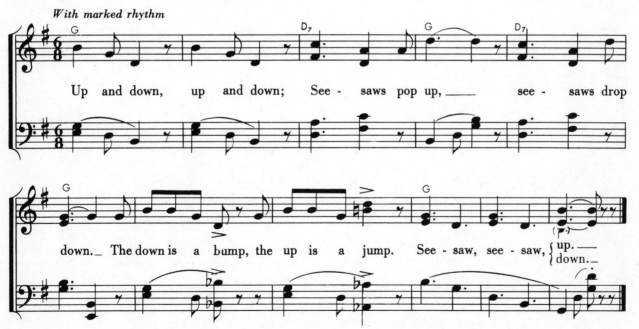

Up and down, up and down; See - saws pop up, ____ see - saws drop

down. __ The down is a bump, the up is a jump. See - saw, see - saw, { up. ____ down. __

Giddy-ap Pony

WORDS BY MARION ABESON
MUSIC BY CHARITY BAILEY

A pony ride in the park! Children are the pony and the rider all at once. Or a pony pulling a cart may seem a good idea. Tone blocks or coconut shells can make the steady "clop clop."

With marked rhythm

1. Gid - dy - ap, po - ny, Clop, clop, clop, clop; Gid - dy - ap,
2. All the little po - nies Trot, trot, trot, trot; All the little

po - ny, Lift that knee. Gid - dy - ap, po - ny,
po - nies Trot in line. Now the little po - nies

Clop, clop, clop, clop; Gid - dy - ap, po - ny, Trot with me.
Feel hot, hot, hot; Trot __ to the brook, It's drink - ing time.

Parallel listening: "High-Stepping Horses," Anderson. RCA Victor Basic Library.
"Trotting Horses," Anderson. RCA Victor Basic Library.

104

It's hard to choose between the up and down motion of riding on a horse or elephant or fish and the round and round motion of the merry-go-round itself as we sing. Here comes the ticket man!

WORDS AND MUSIC BY GEORGE MITCHELL

Oh, how I like to go round and round All day long on a mer-ry-go-round.

Pranc-ing hors-es and kan-ga-roos, Gai-ly gal-lop-ing two by twos.

Oh, how I like to go round and round All day long on a mer-ry-go-round.

105

The Seals

WORDS BY DOROTHY ALDIS
MUSIC BY ERNEST GOLD

One of the biggest crowds in any zoo gathers to watch the seals. Usually there are many seals, all doing different fascinating things. Have you too many "seals?" Some may be onlookers.

The seals all flap their shin-ing flips, And bounce balls on their nos-y tips, And beat a drum, and catch a bar, And wig-gle with how pleased they are.____

Parallel listening: "Let's Play Zoo." Young People's Records.

The Bear

WORDS ANONYMOUS
MUSIC BY ALYS E. BENTLEY

Bears are huge clumsy creatures that children love to imitate. Watch them stand on their hind legs and move about, weaving in and out in a kind of rhythmic movement.

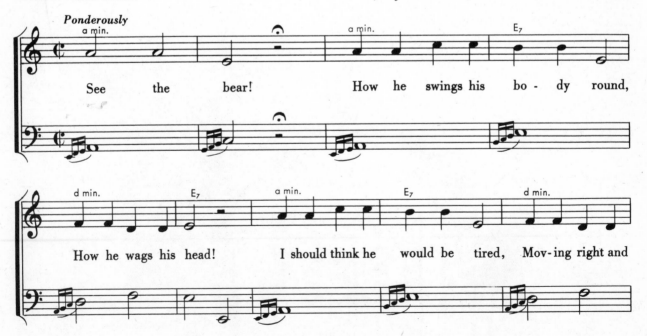

See the bear! How he swings his bo-dy round, How he wags his head! I should think he would be tired, Mov-ing right and

106

mov- ing left.   See   the   bear!

Parallel listening: "The Elephant," from *Carnival of the Animals*, Saint-Saëns.
"Jimbo's Lullaby," from *Children's Corner Suite*. Debussy.
Ⓡ

Almost everywhere children at play invent a game in which, at a set signal, the players freeze in some position. This is good for sharpening ears for a variety of signals.

Jacky Stand Still

DUTCH NURSERY RHYME
TRADITIONAL MELODY

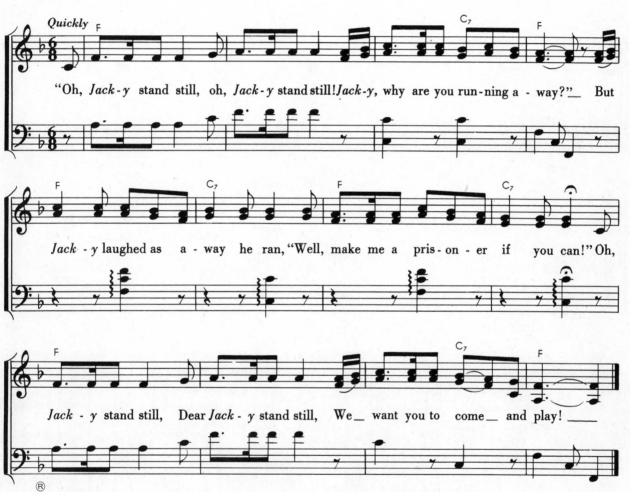

"Oh, *Jack-y* stand still, oh, *Jack-y* stand still! *Jack-y*, why are you run-ning a - way?"_ But

Jack - y laughed as   a - way   he ran, "Well, make me a   pris-on-er   if   you can!" Oh,

Jack - y stand still, Dear *Jack - y* stand still, We_ want you to come_ and play! _____

Ⓡ

Some of the children sing while others play the game of freezing into a statue, on the held note. If a piano is available, words may be omitted until after the held note. Toward the end of the year, the children will have moved in many different ways to different music. Teacher can then play a signal game with the children by switching from one piece to another, without warning.

The Lion

ROGER
NEW YORK CITY SCHOOL

When many animals in the zoo have been drama-tized, try setting up a "zoo." Each cageful of ani-mals begins to move and act their roles when they hear their music played.

Deliberately

Once there was a lion, He walked up and

down the cage. He walked up and down, and up and

down, And up and down the cage. _____

LION

108

The Year Around

6

GAYEST OF ALL

Spring noises: try to
Count how many—
Organs grinding
For a penny.
Balloon men blowing
Up the street.
Peddlers crying
Things to eat.
Shower-spatters,
Skaters, skooters,
Baseball batters,
Marble shooters,
And gayest of all,
The tree-top song
Of robins, robins
All day long.

—Dorothy Aldis

Falling snow . . . sudden spring sunshine . . . the celebration of a holiday . . . children are moved by these things, like to make songs about them or sing the songs other people have made. Holiday music, enjoyed at school, is often carried into the home, where it serves to bring home and school closer together. Here is music for many occasions, the range of which can be extended by inventing new words or sound effects. Familiar songs, piano pieces, and records are all useful in dramatizing a special occasion. See suggested ideas on p. 120.

Hey! Hey!

WORDS ADAPTED
SWISS FOLK TUNE

Verses may be added about other activities under-
taken on a trip to the park . . roller skating or riding
on the merry-go-round.

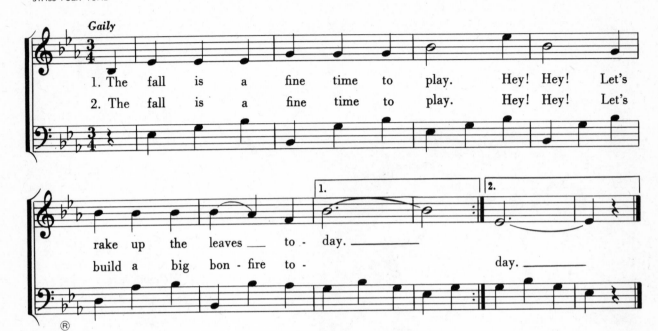

Gaily

1. The fall is a fine time to play. Hey! Hey! Let's
2. The fall is a fine time to play. Hey! Hey! Let's

rake up the leaves ___ to - day. ___
build a big bon - fire to- day. ___

Down, Down!

WORDS BY ELEANOR FARJEON
MUSIC BY ERNEST GOLD

Some of autumn's falling leaves are raked into
piles and burned. For raking, building a bonfire,
and dancing around it, we use "In the Garden,"
p. 42, making the word-changes we need.

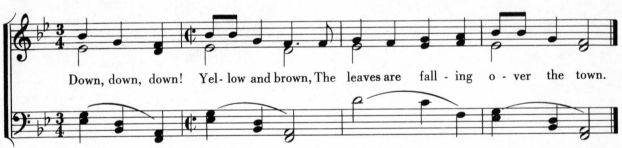

Down, down, down! Yel- low and brown, The leaves are fall - ing o - ver the town.

I Saw a Little Leaf

MARTHA, THOMAS METCALF SCHOOL
NORMAL, ILLINOIS

Each passing season comes as a big event. So we
signalize fall, winter, and spring in turn. The little
leaf thus might be a raindrop on a rainy day or a
snowflake in wintertime.

I saw a lit - tle leaf, It was go - ing round and round.

It whirled and whirled and whirled and whirled; It fell to the ground.

Some may be witches stirring the brew, others are owls on creaking trees, who sway their heads in spooky fashion. We will need to have "tiptoe people," too—goblins, pumpkin men, and cats.

Witches and Owls

WORDS AND MUSIC BY CLARA ELLEN SPELMAN

Parallel listening: "Gnomes," Reinhold. RCA Victor Basic Library.
Parallel listening: "Dwarfs," Reinhold. RCA Victor Basic Library.

The Halloween atmosphere is greatly enhanced by sound effects. Stirring noises are made by rattles or maracas, creaking noises by notched rhythm sticks, creeping or shuffling steps by sand blocks. BOO calls for a crashing cymbal.

Halloween

KATHRYN, THOMAS METCALF SCHOOL
NORMAL, ILLINOIS

111

It's a Pumpkin

WORDS — UNKNOWN
MUSIC BY ARTHUR EDWARDS

With humor

1. It will make a jack-o'-lan-tern, Or a big Thanks-giv-ing pie. It's a big round yel-low some-thing. You can guess it if you try.

Parallel listening: "Clowns," from *Midsummer Night's Dream*, Mendelssohn. RCA Victor Basic Library.

2. We will give it eyes and nose,
And a great big grinning smile.
Then we'll light it with a candle
Jack-o'-lantern! Hold it high.

3. We will cut it up and cook it,
And we'll mix in spices, too.
Then we'll bake it in the oven.
It's a pumpkin pie—for you!

*Thanksgiving would hardly be Thanksgiving with-
out this perennial favorite. Ankle bells add to the
fun when the children become horses prancing off
to grandfather's farm.*

Over the River
and Through the Wood

OLD SONG — WORDS BY LYDIA MARIA CHILDS

Gaily

1. O- ver the riv- er and through the wood, To grand- fa-ther's house we go; ___ The
2. O- ver the riv- er and through the wood, Trot fast, ___ my dap- ple gray! ___ Spring

horse knows the way to car- ry the sleigh Thro' the white and drift- ed snow. ___
ov - er the ground, like a hunt - ing hound, For this is Thanks-giv-ing Day! ___

O - ver the riv- er and through the wood, Oh, how the wind does blow! ___ It
O - ver the riv- er and through the wood, Now grand-mother's face I spy! ___ Hur-

stings the toes and bites the nose, As o- ver the ground we go.
rah for the fun! Is the pud- ding done? Hur- rah for the pump- kin pie!

*What can strengthen home-school relations better
than carrying a song learned at school into the
home to add meaning to a holiday?*

Thankfulness

OLD ENGLISH ROUND

For health and strength and dai - ly food We praise Thy name, O Lord.

My Father's Children

SPIRITUAL

We may sing, after a discussion, "We're thankful for rain and sunshine," or "for food and shelter." Or we sing of ourselves as members of the band, "I am Nathaniel Taylor," etc.

These are my Fa - ther's chil - dren, These are my Fa - ther's chil - dren,

These are my Fa - ther's chil - dren, All _____ in one band.

Mr. Turkey

WORDS ANONYMOUS
MUSIC BY FLORENCE WHITE

The hero of the Thanksgiving occasion is of course the proudly strutting turkey (and the children who move about the room, playing this role). Some think the turkey's "elegance" derives from an appetite that has outgrown the size of his feet.

1. When Mis - ter Tur - key is walk - ing out, What do you think he
2. It does - n't mat - ter what you say, He'll an - swer you the

talks a - bout? Gob - ble, gob - ble, gob - ble. _____
same queer way. Gob - ble, gob - ble, gob - ble. _____

114

A very simple dance may be improvised. As the children sing "la, la," they walk around a circle. At "Torah," they stand still and clap their hands. Bells help first part of song; drums, second part.

Torah Orah

JEWISH FOLK SONG

Refrain

La- la- la- la- la- la- la- la- la- la- la,   La- la- la- la- la   la- la- la- la,

La- la- la- la- la-   la- la- la- la- la,   La- la-   la- la- la- la- la.

Verse

To - rah o - rah,   To - rah o - rah,   hal - le - lu -   jah!

To - rah o - rah,   To - rah o - rah,   hal - le - lu -   jah!

Immediately after the Harvest Festival comes a holiday known as Simhat Torah, or Rejoicing of the Torah. The sacred scrolls of the law are taken out of the Ark and carried around the synagogue, in gay procession. In some very traditional synagogues, people dance with the scrolls in their arms. The word "Torah" literally refers to the Five Books of Moses contained in the scrolls. It usually has the broader connotation of law, learning, good life.

115

The Cat in the Snow

TRADITIONAL SONG

It's fun to make tracks in wet sand or damp earth or with wet feet on the floor, as well as in the snow. Children then look at different tracks, compare them, and play them on instruments.

Oh! Oh! Oh! The cat is in the snow! She

gets her snow-y leg-gings on as soon as she be-gins to run. Oh, dear-y oh! Oh, dear-y oh! The cat is in the snow!

Parallel listening: "Capering Kittens," Ganz. Decca.
"Snow Is Dancing," from *Children's Corner Suite*, Debussy.

One group of children traced the pattern of their mittens on paper and colored them. Some were like the originals—others brand new designs. These were proudly exhibited as this song was sung.

The Mitten Song

WORDS BY MARIE LOUISE ALLEN
MUSIC BY ERNEST GOLD

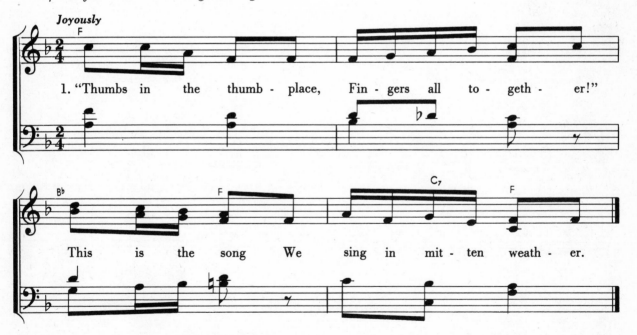

1. "Thumbs in the thumb-place, Fin-gers all to-geth-er!" This is the song We sing in mit-ten weath-er.

2. When it is cold,
   It doesn't matter whether
   Mittens are wool,
   Or made of finest leather.

3. This is the song
   We sing in mitten-weather;
   "Thumbs in the thumb-place,
   Fingers all together!"

On This Night

WORDS BY S. S. GROSSMAN
MUSIC BY S. E. GOLDFARB

Hanukah, the Festival of Lights, lasts eight days. One candle of the Menorah is lit the first night; each night one more is added. The number in the song should be changed as song is dramatized.

On this night, let us light One lit-tle can-dle fire; ___

'Tis a sight, Oh, so bright! One lit-tle can-dle fire. ___

Jingle Bells

WORDS AND MUSIC BY J. PIERPONT

Wearing wristlets or anklets of bells, or a sash of bells around the waist, or carrying jingle bells, children trot to this song while others sing it.

Jin-gle bells! Jin-gle bells! Jin-gle all the way!

Oh, what fun it is to ride in a one-horse o-pen sleigh! ___

Jin-gle bells! Jin-gle bells! Jin-gle all the way!

Oh, what fun it is to ride in a one-horse o-pen sleigh!

Christmas Chant

ARRANGED BY E. T. COOK
GREGORIAN

Comes the Christmas season, ushered in by a melody dating back to 450 A.D.—long before music had been strait-jacketed into major or minor.

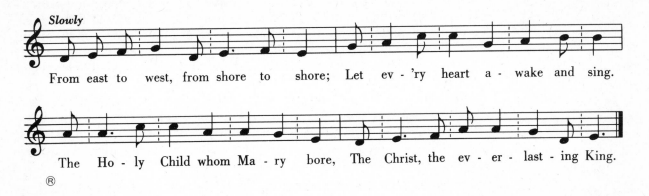

Slowly

From east to west, from shore to shore; Let ev - 'ry heart a - wake and sing.

The Ho - ly Child whom Ma - ry bore, The Christ, the ev - er - last - ing King.

Away in a Manger

WORDS BY MARTIN LUTHER
MUSIC BY CARL MÜLLER

This Christmas song, well-loved by children, comes from a much later period, when simple people first began to sing along with the choir in the churches.

Tenderly

1. A - way in a man - ger, no crib for a bed, The lit - tle Lord
2. The cat - tle are low - ing, the poor Ba - by wakes, But lit - tle Lord

Je - sus laid down His sweet head; The stars in the sky ___ looked
Je - sus no cry - ing He makes; I love Thee, Lord Je - sus! Look

down where He lay, The lit - tle Lord Je - sus, a - sleep on the hay.
down from the sky, And stay by my cra - dle, till morn - ing is nigh.

119

Santa's Helpers. Early in the season every child will want to help Santa finish the toys for his pack, making sure there are enough for every girl and boy. All the "toy" songs may be reviewed (pp. 39-41). "My goodness, Santa hasn't had time to put the lids on the Jack-in-the-boxes. Let's saw up some wood for him" ("Sawing Firewood," p. 59). Any song, piano piece, or record in marching rhythm is good for hammering nails. Little nails need short, quick strokes; big nails slower, harder strokes. (Groups of black keys on the piano make excellent nails). Toys need painting, too, ("A Work Chant," p. 24). Later, when all is ready, toys are packed and Santa's bag loaded in his sleigh ("Jigglity-Jogglety," p. 102). Of course, Santa supervises the job ("Ha, Ha, This-a-Way," p. 6). Off he goes in his sleigh pulled by galloping reindeer. "Jingle Bells" (p. 118) will be useful here, or a gallop played on piano or phonograph. Christmas-tree trimming (dramatized) will review many songs, especially "O Christmas Tree." Under our tree we cradle the Christchild, using all the lullabies we know.

Las Posadas. Or we may share the quite different customs of a Mexican Christmas. Every night, in the weeks before Christmas, candle-lit processions, singing litanies, go from house to house seeking lodgings *(posadas)*, as Mary and Joseph did at Bethlehem. The neighbor whose turn it is to entertain stays home, pretends to refuse admission, but finally yields. After devotions before the *creche* there is merry-making and the breaking of the *piñata*, a decorated clay jar full of sweets. Someone is blindfolded; the *piñata* is dangled out of reach of his stick; then, after he has swung wildly, he is allowed to hit it, and all scramble for the contents.

Las Posadas Songs

MEXICAN CHRISTMAS SONG
COLLECTED BY NATIVIDAD VACIO

MEXICAN CHRISTMAS SONG

⟨see above⟩

120

As we circle round our tree, we sing the song that is as much a part of Christmas as the Christmas tree itself.

O Christmas Tree

GERMAN FOLK SONG

In a stately manner

O Christ-mas tree, O Christ-mas tree,

How ev - er - green your branch - es!

1. You nev - er change the whole year 'round,
2. We trim the tree at Christ-mas time,

You bright-en up the snow - y ground.
And mer - ry bells be - gin to chime.

O Christ-mas tree, O Christ-mas tree, How ev - er - green your branch - es!

Holiday Song

WORDS AND MUSIC BY NELLIE KAVELIN

This, of course, may be "New Year's Day is such a jolly time," or my birthday, or Halloween, or any other holiday that needs a happy song.

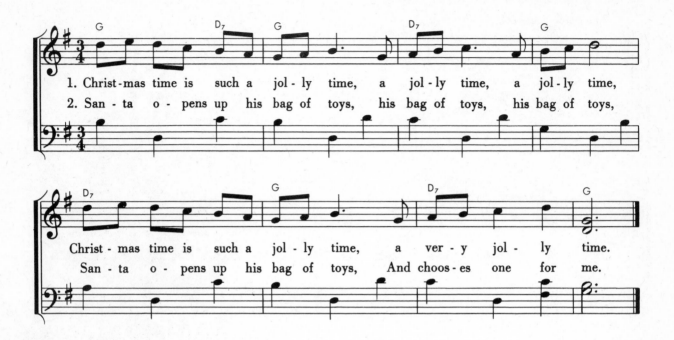

1. Christ-mas time is such a jol-ly time, a jol-ly time, a jol-ly time,
2. San-ta o-pens up his bag of toys, his bag of toys, his bag of toys,

Christ-mas time is such a jol-ly time, a ver-y jol-ly time.
San-ta o-pens up his bag of toys, And choos-es one for me.

Merry Bells of Christmas Ring

SATIS N. COLEMAN AND ALICE G. THORN

Play this song slowly and heavily at a lower pitch and children will respond by tugging hard to sound tremendous bells. Play it lightly and higher and children will ring tiny, jingly bells.

The mer-ry bells of Christ-mas ring, Ding, dong, ding, dong, And

joy to all the chil-dren bring, Ding, dong, ding!

Parallel listening: "Legend of the Bells," from *Chimes of Normandy*. RCA Victor Basic Library.

There are many well-known carols for singing. Here is a carol traditionally for dancing and singing both. The children will enjoy making up their own special dance to this music.

Now It Is Christmas

SWEDISH DANCE CAROL

"When it is Easter time," the words of this song are turned around to suit the season and we sing "happy days we'll have till Christmas. Then it is Christmas time, and then it is Christmas time, and happy days we'll have till Easter."

Christmas is a season of hospitality and sharing. Children like to invite their mothers to come to school to sing the Christmas songs, to play rhythm instruments (with the children offering instruction, proudly), and to share the fun of the dramatizations. Parents usually enjoy this sort of spontaneous program that mirrors the daily music time in the classroom far more than a rehearsed performance gotten up specially for the occasion.

Glory, Glory, Hallelujah!

WORDS BY JULIA WARD HOWE
MUSIC BY WILLIAM STEFFE

First graders like to help the older children sing at assemblies celebrating the birthdays of Lincoln and Washington. Their faces beam with pleasure as they join in this simple refrain.

Glo - ry, glo - ry, hal - le - lu - jah! Glo - ry, glo - ry, hal - le - lu - jah!

Glo - ry, glo - ry, hal - le - lu - jah! His truth is march - ing on.

Yankee Doodle

TRADITIONAL WORDS
OLD TUNE

The pony may trot or it may prance, while the parade marches along, paper hats aloft and drums stirring.

Yan - kee Doo - dle came to town, rid - ing on a po - ny;

Stuck a feath - er in his cap, and called it "Mac - a - ro - ni."

124

Refrain

Yan - kee Doo - dle, keep it up, Yan - kee Doo - dle dan - dy,

Mind the mu - sic and the step, and with the girls be hand - y.

Here is another song six-year-olds will want to sing with parents and older brothers and sisters.

America

WORDS BY SAMUEL FRANCIS SMITH
MUSIC BY HENRY CAREY

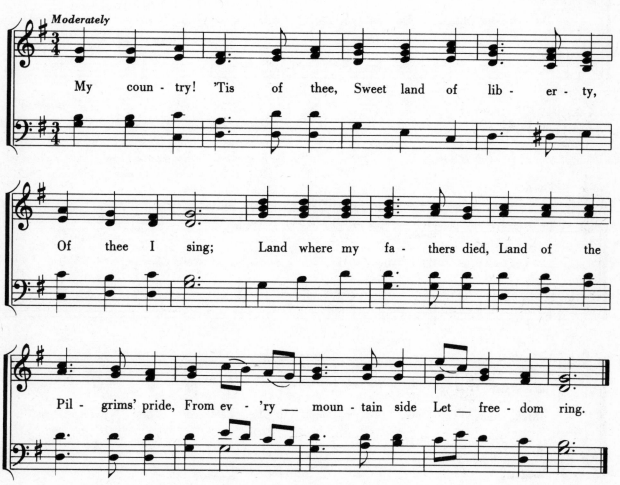

Moderately

My coun - try! 'Tis of thee, Sweet land of lib - er - ty,

Of thee I sing; Land where my fa - thers died, Land of the

Pil - grims' pride, From ev - 'ry ___ moun - tain side Let ___ free - dom ring.

Valentine Song

WORDS ADAPTED
MUSIC BY NELLIE KAVELIN

By changing a word here and there, we can adapt many a song to some special need or occasion. Notice how this song for Valentine's Day has been made from "Holiday Song," p. 122.

1. I will make a val-en-tine for you, A val-en-tine, a val-en-tine,
2. I will write on it, "I love you true, I love you true, I love you true."

I will make a val-en-tine for you, All trimmed with lace and flowers.
I will write on it, "I love you true, Please be my val-en-tine."

Dayeynu

TRADITIONAL PASSOVER SONG

Sacred days marking release from bondage come as spring breaks the grip of winter's cold. This traditional song of thanks is sung at the Passover table. "Dayeynu" is pronounced Dy-yea-noo.

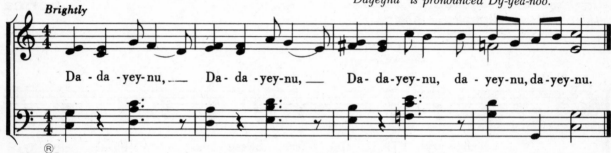

Brightly

Da-da-yey-nu,___ Da-da-yey-nu,___ Da-da-yey-nu, da-yey-nu, da-yey-nu.

Easter Eggs

WORDS AND MUSIC BY GRACE M. MESERVE

Easter, another spring holy day, is symbolized by eggs and the chick bursting the bonds of a shell. Easter also means bunnies and a new wardrobe. Use "The Hatman," p. 94, and "The Rabbit," p. 70.

Lively

(Whisper)
One - two - three - four - five - six - seven - eight. One, two,

(Sing)
three, four, five, six, sev-en, eight lit-tle East-er eggs. Green, red,

126

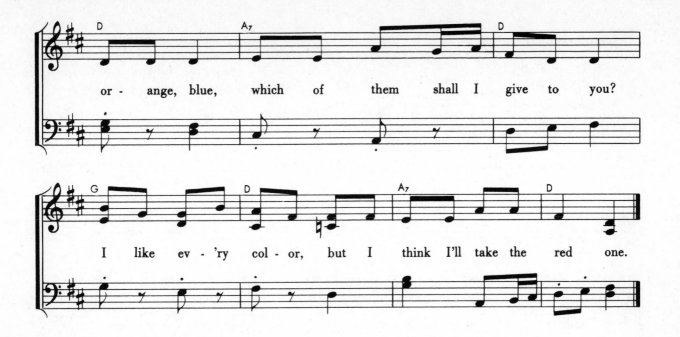

or - ange, blue, which of them shall I give to you?

I like ev - 'ry col - or, but I think I'll take the red one.

Yes, April showers do bring May flowers—and dripping umbrellas and lost rubbers and the smell of wet wool. Well . . . one can always remember that at six rain and mud seemed lots of fun.

Mud

WORDS BY POLLY CHASE BOYDEN
MUSIC BY MILTON KAYE

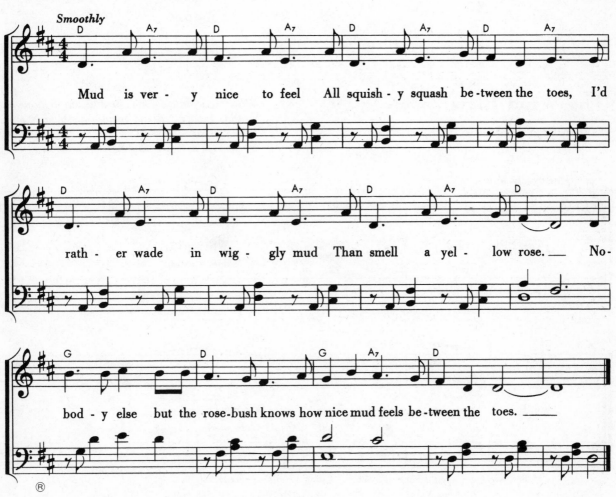

Smoothly

Mud is ver - y nice to feel All squish - y squash be - tween the toes, I'd

rath - er wade in wig - gly mud Than smell a yel - low rose. __ No-

bod - y else but the rose-bush knows how nice mud feels be - tween the toes. ____

I Like Rain

WORDS BY ADINA WILLIAMSON
MUSIC BY FLORENCE WHITE

The tinkling sound of the triangle goes well with this song. Children may also enjoy patterning on this instrument the actual beating of the rain upon the windowpane, some rainy spring day.

1. I like rain, I like the wa-ter in the streets,
2. I like rain, I like the way it drops and roots Out
3. I like rain, Then moth-er makes up gin-ger-bread,

And the way it beats and beats Up-on the win-dow-pane.
pud-dles for my big rain boots To splash a splash-ing game.
Hon-ey cakes for me to spread, A-cross a sheet of rain.

Parallel listening: "Raindrops" from Songs for Young Harpists, Salzedo.

The Wind Blew East

FOLK SONG FROM THE BAHAMAS

What the wind blew may be adapted to locale and season. In the fall the wind may blow the red leaves or tumbleweed; in winter, the snowflakes or sleet; in summer, thunderclouds or dust.

Oh, the wind blew east, Whoooo! _____ The
(imitate wind)

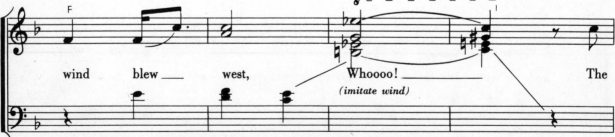

wind blew ____ west, Whoooo! _____ The
(imitate wind)

Parallel listening: "My Playmate the Wind." Young People's Records.

128

wind blew the sun-shine Right down to town.

Refrain

Oh, the wind blew the sun-shine Right__ down to

town, Oh, the wind blew the sun-shine Right__ down to town.

We know fall has really come when we need wraps out-of-doors. We know spring has come (to most latitudes) when we're sure we can leave them off— only to discover we're chilly.

Hat and Coat

WORDS AND MUSIC BY ERNEST GOLD

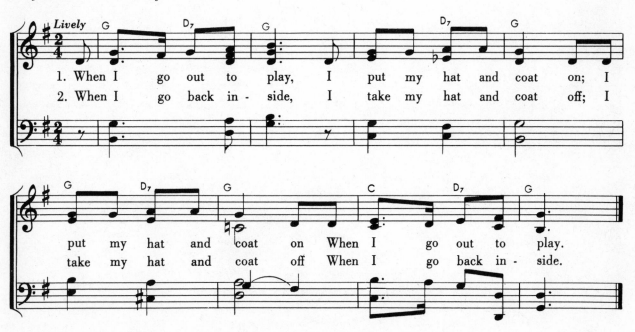

1. When I go out to play, I put my hat and coat on; I
2. When I go back in-side, I take my hat and coat off; I

put my hat and coat on When I go out to play.
take my hat and coat off When I go back in-side.

Spring Is Coming

WORDS — UNKNOWN
MUSIC BY MILTON KAYE

Little Johnny-jump-up said,
"It must be spring.
I just saw a lady bug
And heard a robin sing."
—EDWINNA FALLIS

Liltingly

1. Spring is com - ing, spring is com - ing, How do you think I know? _____ I
2. Summer is com - ing, summer is com - ing, How do you think I know? _____ A

found some pus - sy wil - lows; I know it must be so.
black - eyed Su - san winked at me; I know it must be so.

3. Autumn is coming,
   Autumn is coming,
   How do you think I know?
   A yellow leaf just fluttered by;
   I know it must be so.

4. Winter is coming,
   Winter is coming,
   How do you think I know?
   I felt a snowflake tickle my nose;
   I know it must be so.

130

Sometimes it's fun to go for a walk to music that
teacher plays on the piano. Piano music is useful
for prolonging activities initiated by the singing of
a song or for accompanying a brand new activity.
It may be the postman who walks to this piece.
When he's tired, play it in a minor key.

Out for a Walk

OPUS 119, NO. 12
ALEXANDER GRETCHANINOFF

Gigue

ADAPTED FROM SUITE NO. 3
ARCANGELO CORELLI

Different kinds of music call for different types of activity. This music will make the children think of skipping, bouncing balls, rowing boats, or paddling canoes.

Tarantelle

OPUS 65
SERGE PROKOFIEFF

This music calls for galloping, hopping, whirling, for rolling hoops, for dramatizing rolling tumbleweed or any other rolling thing in the children's environment.

132

133

Ländler

OPUS 67
FRANZ SCHUBERT

Here is music for stamping, pushing and pulling, broad jumping, ball bouncing, wading in water, mud or snow, raking, spading or digging, pitching hay or being a bulldozer.

With marked accents

134

Round Dance

VOLUME 1, NO. 10
BELA BARTOK

On rainy days we may want to dramatize the dancing raindrops, or, in winter, the whirling of snowflakes against our windowpane. Sometimes, again, it's fun just to run or play tag to music.

Theme from Kinderstücke

OPUS 72, NO. 2
FELIX MENDELSSOHN

Children need music that induces repose as well as rhythmic activity. Teacher finds it handy to have some music that quiets her children—rests them before going into a new activity.

Sleighride

OPUS 57
HERMANN ZILCHER

Some children will be the sleigh, others riders, and proudest of all will be the trotting horses. There will be other jobs for trotting horses, too, such as pulling wagons or carrying riders in the park.

136

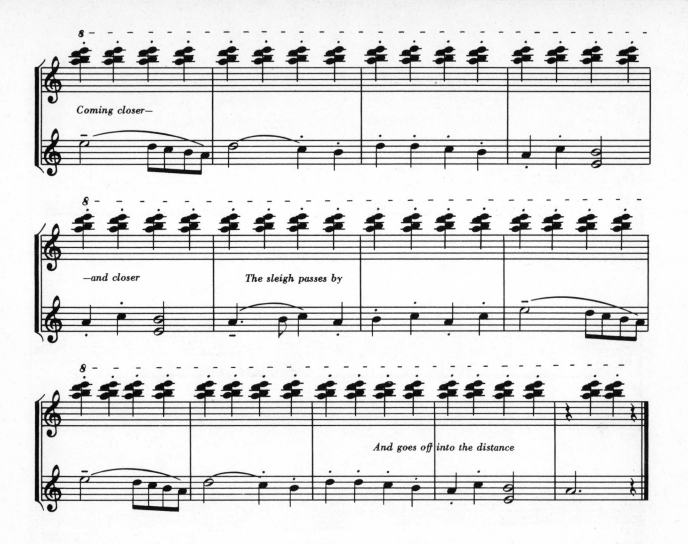

Coming closer—

—and closer

The sleigh passes by

And goes off into the distance

This waltz tune is good for rocking movements. Good, too, for tossing up real or imaginary balloons which are pushed up again and again, on successive strong pulses in the music.

Waltz

OPUS 39, NO. 2
JOHANNES BRAHMS

A Little Joke

DMITRI KABALEVSKY

Children like to be clowns tumbling to this music.
Or they may be clouds scudding across the sky, or
jack-o'-lanterns, or wind-tossed kites, or—perhaps
—just skating, sliding girls and boys.

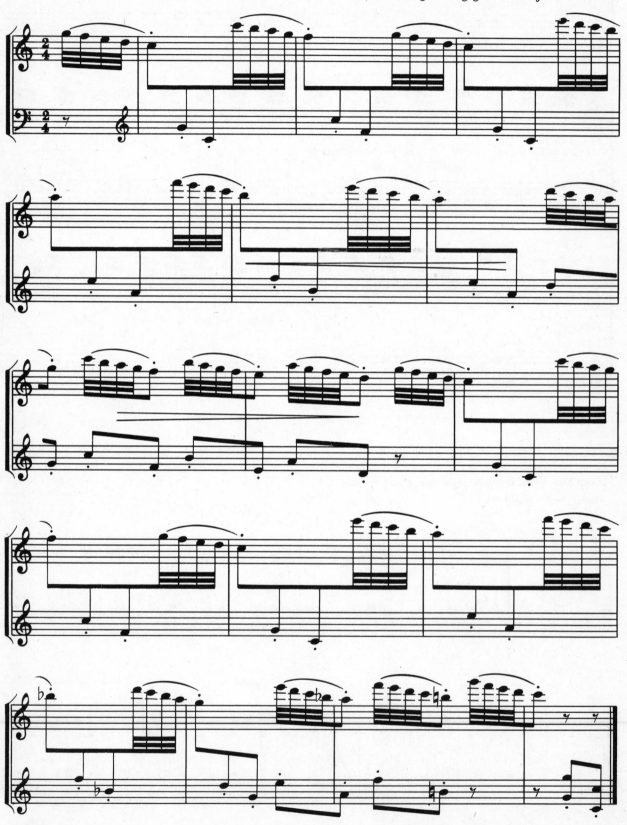

138

This music suggests being bears or elephants or other heavy animals — perhaps big work horses pulling heavy loads. Or we may pretend to wade in slush or puddles with our sloshing galoshes on.

March

ALEXIS HOLLAENDER
(ABRIDGED)

Marche

J. S. BACH

It's fun, when marching, to look back over one's shoulder at our column of boys and girls, to see what "shape" we've made. Sometimes we forget ourselves and become strutting geese or turkeys.

Plants Growing

ERNEST GOLD

After observing the growth of bulbs in the class-room, or plants out-of-doors, we dramatize all the successive stages of growth. Or perhaps we're cocoons turning into butterflies.

We may be butterflies or birds soaring. In winter
we may lie on our backs and make "angels" in the
"snow," or pedal bicycle wheels. Or we may paint
the house or play merry-go-round.

Papillons

OPUS 2, NO. 8
ROBERT SCHUMANN

Arran Boat Song

SCOTTISH MELODY

Boats, too, capture the imagination. Here is music for rocking, swaying, being boats, waves, and bell-buoys. For ringing big bells, too, and for being flying birds or swaying trees.

A Letter to Teacher

DEAR TEACHER:

We hope that you and your children will enjoy this book we have prepared. But beyond this, we hope that all of you will gain solid benefits from it. We believe you can. That is what this letter is about.

Nothing would please us better than to visit your classrooms and sit down and talk over your work with you. During such a visit we could discuss ways in which our book might be helpful to you. We, ourselves, would learn a great deal from such a situation, as all of us have done many a time. And perhaps for you, too, some useful ideas would come from our discussion of matters, together. But since this is impossible, a letter will have to do!

We want to tell you something of how we have made this book, why we chose the music in it, why it is arranged as it is, and also to suggest some ways of using it with your children. We realize, of course, that you will think of other ways that haven't occurred to us. Also we hope to indicate how the book can be used with pleasure and profit to *you*, for we are quite convinced that a teacher's satisfaction is very important. In everything we say, we will try to be PRACTICAL.

What is the most practical thing for any teacher? It is his POINT OF VIEW, for this influences everything he does. We are sure you will agree that this is so; in preparing this book we have found it very true indeed. For without a definite point of view to guide us, we wouldn't have known how to go about our job.

Our point of view is this: THE MOST VITAL THING A TEACHER CAN DO FOR A CHILD IS TO HELP HIM GROW UP PROPERLY . . . to grow up mentally, socially, emotionally, spiritually . . . to grow up into a good, a useful, a well-adjusted person.

But what has this got to do with the matter? This is a fair question. Here is our answer. We are convinced that music can do a great deal—indeed an amazing great deal—to help a child grow up properly. Our book is planned to help you use music for just this purpose; we are sure that you will find a real joy in using music in this way.

This central point of view of ours leads to a number of questions which we shall try to answer in the following pages. You will find that much of this answer lies in the nature of music itself.

First, in exactly *what ways* can music help a child to grow up? We have thought of ten such ways, all related to the uses of this book.

Second, *what kind of musical experiences* should a child have if he is to grow up through music? Here we shall have suggestions about listening, singing, playing, rhythmic activities, and creative experiences.

Third, how can we help a child to *discover things* about music for himself? We shall consider the advantages to be gained when he has a book of his own in his hands, in which he may revel and also make observations.

Fourth, what about *musical growth itself*? Music can help a child to grow up; but how much will he learn about music itself, in the process? This is a very important question, to which we think we have found a satisfactory answer.

We hope you will find our suggestions interesting and helpful, and that they will aid you in using our book for the central purpose we have in mind. We believe that they will help you to find real pleasure in bringing music to your children.

With very best wishes,

James L. Mursell
Gladys Tipton
Beatrice Landeck
Harriet Nordholm
Roy E. Freeburg
Jack M. Watson

TEN WAYS OF GROWING UP

As we told you, we have thought of ten ways in which a child grows up. We believe we can see how music can help with all of them. Of course a child doesn't grow up in these ten ways separately, one by one. They all go on together. But for the sake of clear thinking, it is helpful to single them out.

1 *A child grows up by gaining a sense of personal worth and self-confidence.* His feeling that "he is somebody," that "he amounts to something," is vastly important for his whole development.

Here music can help. A child finds that he can sing, or play an instrument, or suggest a new verse or a good dramatization, and that these are very enjoyable experiences. Won't this help his self-confidence? Of course it will.

2 *A child grows up by developing his ability to deal with other people and to get along with them well.* Again, music can help. In this book you will find a wealth of opportunities for many kinds of co-operation. Dramatizations, choosing instrumental effects, suggesting new words, calling attention to sound effects, playing games, taking the lead as soloists, joining in with small groups, playing games —all these are chances to learn the great lesson of getting on with others. Some of the subject divisions in Chapter One may call such opportunities to your attention. But these are only hints, starting points for your thinking; chances for cooperation occur all through the book.

3 *Children grow up by discovering the pleasure of success.* Here music offers wonderful opportunities. One of our firmest convictions is that every child can succeed with music and that such success is delightful. So all our songs are chosen to encourage children to sing and to like to sing. Also there are simple instruments to be played, rhythmic and dramatic interpretations to be invented and enjoyed, many opportunities for ideas, suggestions, initiative to come bubbling forth creatively.

4 *A child grows up in and through bodily movement.* One might say that children think, feel, and savor their experiences in and through movement. Musical accompaniment enhances rhythmic bodily expression.

Music goes hand in hand with movement. To move rhythmically and expressively to music is to experience it in a very vital way; the experience does

something to the entire personality. So all through this book there are opportunities for free, expressive, creative movement. The material under "Hand Games" (p. 4) and "Rhythmic Activities" (p. 7) will show you what is meant, although it is only a sample.

5 *Rest and relaxation are very important for development.* The tensions and pressures of the school day bear heavily on young children and can be harmful. Here again music can help, for one of its most universal effects is its soothing, calming influence. If you examine the book, including the index, you will find that this has been provided for.

6 *A child grows up by dramatizing his experiences.* In doing this, he grasps the meaning of an experience very vividly. You and I often dramatize our experiences for just this reason. Remember that dramatization has a much greater role with children than with adults. So in this book you will find much encouragement for children to dramatize the experiences to which the music is related, by responding creatively, by inventing their own ways of acting out the experience concerned.

7 *A child grows up through a developing sense of the people and things around him, and of their meaning;* through a discovery, ever wider and deeper, of the realities about him, and of their wonder and appeal.

Here again music can help. Music is not isolated from life and reality. It is a sort of comment on things, people, events—an interpretation of their emotional meanings. So the music of this book is related to the realities among which the child lives. It is concerned with home and toys and pets, with city streets and country scenes, with passing seasons, and with land and sea and sky. All this you will see from chapter titles and song titles.

8 *A child grows up by finding new ways of expressing himself.* Ideas and feelings are clarified— one might almost say realized and actualized—in and through expression.

So, in this book, music and its companion art of poetry are treated as means of expression. The child finds that, through music, he can say something about familiar things like his puppy, the family car, the bus, the kitchen cupboard, and also about remoter things like ships, lighthouses, wind, and stars.

9 *A child grows up by discovering the many fascinating realities of the world of sound.* These realities are not limited to musical sound itself. Thus we have provided many opportunities for children to develop an awareness of a wide range of sound-values—the sounds made by machines, natural forces such as rain and wind, and the tones of the human voice. Then, too, we have provided for a wide range of instrumental effects with which children can experiment and among which they can choose. The section "Getting Acquainted with Instruments," beginning p. 16, may be helpful as a starting point.

10 *Children grow by bringing their experiences, actions, and responses more and more under meaningful control.* They grow by gaining the ability to control their responses by numbers, words, concepts, general principles.

The same is true with music. Children can realize more and more that the charm and expressiveness of music depends on organized form that can be designated by names and symbols—that a tone can be high and low, that a melody rises and falls, that a phrase begins and ends, that rhythms have definable shapes, that chords which produce different effects have different names, and so on. Music cannot fully serve as a means of over-all, inclusive personal development unless this growth in control through meaning and insight takes place.

MUSIC CAN HELP

Listening

There are many ways for children to listen to music.

1. *Attentive listening.* Children listen to a record right through at least once and then interpret it dramatically or by a rhythmic movement. Such interpretation should be spontaneous and child-chosen, with the teacher guiding and encouraging, but not imposing his own interpretation.

2. *Quiet listening,* primarily for inner response.

3. *Background listening,* with music as a background for rest periods or quieter classroom activities such as painting, building with large blocks, or gathering at desks or tables as school begins. Longer records can be used here, preferably those not inviting active rhythmic response.

4. *Live talent.* Children may gain much from listening to each other, to older children, to parents, to musical visitors.

Singing

Treat singing as a very personal act and a natural act, depending on confidence, enjoyment, and the urge to sing far more than on any alleged "proper" use of the voice. Here are some points to have in mind in helping children to sing:

1. *Song-inviting tunes.* An attractive tune does wonders in encouraging a child to sing. Give him every chance to enjoy it and let him pick it up little by little, without forcing. Remember that children sing tune-wise rather than notewise, so that the tune should be picked up as a whole, not learned note by note. Control of pitch will develop in time.

2. *Song-inviting ideas.* In any good song, words and music are closely united. Help children to understand and feel the words they are singing. This will help them to sing as they should. A real feeling for the lyric can help not only with the expression (loud, soft, fast, slow), but even with the up-and-down of the melody and with the rhythm.

3. *A song-inviting situation.* Imitating natural or instrumental sounds or making up words can help to put children at their ease with singing. It is often excellent for children to sing alone, or with chosen friends, or in small groups. Beware of singling out individuals for special "help," which often means special discouragement. Let children sing in a normal, natural situation, without special "singing seats." Encourage a vital expressive tone, rather than one that is artificially hushed. Remember that young children tend to sing on a rather low pitch-level, so that higher singing should come as a natural development and not through forcing.

Rhythmic Movement

1. *Use all the space you have.* Rhythm is best grasped through large, coordinated, free-flowing movements, rather than small jerky ones. So use all the classroom space you can for rhythmic movement, so as to give children maximum freedom. Usually they should all move in the same general direction, but this is the only limitation.

2. *Free movement.* Watch for the free, unstudied movements of the children, and from time to time put in a musical accompaniment. Piano is excellent and so are many kinds of simple, easy instruments. Rhythm sticks for running, the tap of a tambourine for skipping, a drum or tom-tom for walking, coconut shells for galloping, and so forth.

3. *Rhythmic response to music played or sung.* Go through the selection while the children listen. They decide on the kind of movement, then go into action. Different children may choose different

movement-patterns. This is all to the good. The section "Rhythmic Activities" (p. 7, Chapter One) will start you off with some suitable music, but a great many pieces and other songs are entirely suitable. Indeed, one may often introduce a song for rhythmic response, then develop it for singing.

4. *Further points.* When you accompany free rhythms, remember that children respond at a faster tempo than adults. If you use the piano, play lightly and with little pedal. Vary your accompaniments, so as not to use always the same music with the same rhythm. A sequence from very vigorous, moderately vigorous, to complete relaxation works out well.

Instruments

As a starting point for your thinking you will find material involving the use of instruments in Chapter One. But this is only intended as an introduction to the idea; opportunities for instrumental effects occur all through the book.

1. *Rhythm instruments*, such as rhythm sticks, tom-toms, coconut shells, etc., should be treated as musical instruments, not mere noise-makers. Let children experiment with them singly, then with a few together, discovering that each has its own "voice" and can produce many different effects. They can be played loud or soft. Often they can be played high or low (rhythm sticks played close to the hands or on ends). They can give a thick or thin sound-texture (rhythm sticks held tightly or loosely). Their sound can be brief or protracted (tone blocks compared to a triangle). A drum sounds differently tapped on center or edge of head or on its side.

In using rhythm instruments with songs, let the children decide which are most suitable. Often you may find it well to delimit the scope of choice to avoid bewilderment. "In this song do we want something that clicks or that rings?" Such questions help the children to choose well. In any case, don't have too many instruments going at once, for the important thing is for children to listen discriminatingly to their effects.

2. *Melody bells* can be used for children to improvise accompaniments (without too much regard for specific notes, so long as they play lightly); or to furnish an introduction or a coda; or to play familiar songs; or to play melodic fragments found in "I Like the City" or "I Like the Country." Tuned water glasses can substitute for or supplement melody bells, in which case let the children help tune them. Melody bells hung on the board or wall give children a visual picture of high and low; water glasses afford a visualization of the scale.

3. Children can do some interesting things with the *piano*; playing it with the forearm, starting with the wrist, and sweeping the arm down on the keys till the elbow touches, or making a glissando with the thumbnail. Up-and-down glissandi can depict a seesaw; animal and bird calls can be played in treble or bass; the rise in pitch as a truck speeds up can be represented. Interesting tunes can be invented on the black keys alone.

4. By all means let the children share in the real pleasure of using the *autoharp*. You may need to help by holding down the bars while the children strum. With ingenuity, some novel sound effects are possible, e.g., the sound of rain by gently swishing the strings. And of course, the autoharp offers an excellent means for grasping the basic chord effects informally and by ear. The autoharp chords indicated in this book outline these basic chord effects. When these have been grasped, it is interesting to use the piano accompaniments, too, which often go beyond these basic chords to achieve a richer effect.

In all that has been said, creative response has been indicated and implied again and again. Now let us consider it directly.

Creative Response

When a child decides that skipping or sliding is the right rhythmic response for a song; when he chooses rhythm sticks for the clicking of car wheels over rails, or low-pitched drum beats for an elephant's tread; when he highlights a melodic fragment on melody bells; when he realizes within himself the calm finality of one chord or the thrusting effect of another; when he realizes that he too can sing, or suggests new words for one song or a dramatization for another—*then that child is behaving creatively.* For a creative response is, simply, one that comes from within, that expresses the child's own initiative and intention as a person. This is the kind of response to stimulate and foster.

All of us, adults and children alike, learn and grow by responding creatively, and only by responding creatively. So, in all that you do with music with your children, whether it be the singing of songs, the playing of instruments, the projection of rhythmic movement, the achieving of dramatizations, encourage initiative, encourage genuine choosing, encourage genuine deciding. In a word, encourage creative response. This means creative teaching on your part, for you must devise opportunities and find ways to help and encourage; and you must beware of imposing your way instead of helping the children to find the way for themselves. You will find such teaching deeply rewarding; and you may be confident that, because of it, the children will grow both musically and as persons.

147

CHILDREN'S MUSIC BOOKS

There can be real value in a child having a music book of his own. Long before they can read, children love to look at books in which the pictures tell the story. Good pictures can widen the horizons of a child, can fill in details beyond his experience. Two "song-story-picture books" have thus been prepared for the children's own hands, "I Like the City" and "I Like the Country."

In these books, songs from "Music Through the Day" have been arranged in story sequence, with other materials added. Browsing through such a book, children are stimulated to dramatic action—their own best way of really learning a song.

One main point of all this is to encourage them to explore the range and qualities of their singing voices and thus become at ease with singing. Thus, in addition to the songs, opportunities are offered for calling animals for feeding, for imitating various environmental sounds—the wind, the street vendor, the siren on the fire truck.

In General

These two books have been planned for informal use and enjoyment, decidedly not for drill. Yet there are many musical elements to be picked up along the way. As children become familiar with the songs, they can be asked to recognize them in their books, by identifying a word, picture, or, in some cases, by the general appearance of the score.

Some children may want to play some of the songs by ear, on instruments. Melody bells will be excellent for this; in some cases the piano is a possibility. "Merrily We Roll Along" (City book, p. 10), for instance, may be played on the black keys of the piano, starting on A-sharp.

Musical Snippets

The "musical snippets"—little fragments of melody or suggested sound effects—are a feature of these books. They can be used in various ways.

Children may like to play them by ear on melody bells or piano (without actually spelling out the notes). Musical snippets derived from familiar songs may be recognized by ear. If a few children recognize them by eye, that's fine; but don't rush this. Children and teacher can make up additional snippets when appropriate, taking them from various songs, or thinking of additional animal calls, bird songs, machine sounds, and so forth.

When reading or telling the stories in the books, let your voice approximate the higher and lower pitches of the musical snippets, rather than stopping to get the exact pitch. Keep these pitch changes as a natural part of the story, as you tell it.

Musical Elements

The children's books were carefully planned to present certain musical elements through picture, story, or musical snippet. The story helps the child not only to see what is there, but to act it out, and thus to understand it.

1. Children need to discover that pitch can be *high* or *low*. Various animal or bird calls, or the contrasting sounds of cars and trucks will help here. So will simple dramatizations of "Kitty in the tree, the robins on the ground," or "Daddy on the hay wagon, Rover and I on the ground."

2. Another idea for children to grasp is that pitch *moves up and down*. The elevator, the slide, the sound of the wind or the siren all help to put this across. Going beyond the books, you can associate the idea with escalators, jet planes, climbing up a ladder and down again, and so on indefinitely. Autumn leaves "dropping" on a flannel board can further illustrate the "downward" idea.

3. Sometimes, too, pitch *stays the same*. This idea is represented by the ding-ding of the fire bell, the zing-zing of sledge hammers, the yip-yip of Rover. Or you may think of dramatizing a tight-rope walker, or climbing a jungle gym for a combination of high-low, up-down, and stay-the-same.

4. The book contains many rhythm patterns, some of which are repetitive, and thus are the basis of *meter* in music. Thus we may do various farm chores while singing "I Want To Be a Farmer." Then we have sawing wood, feeding chickens, raking, sledge hammer pounding, and others.

5. Many rhythms are *uneven*, i.e. combinations of *long* and *short*, like skipping compared to walking. The picture on p. 116 of this book (Country book, 33), illustrates this idea. (Of course, there can be tracks in sand as well as in the snow.)
LOOK: Whose tracks are these? Big or little? Long or short steps? Evenly or unevenly spaced? Daddy's steps are long; mine shorter. Shortest of all are those of little snow sparrows. When I walk my tracks are even. When a bunny hops or a pony gallops, some tracks are wider-spaced than others.
LISTEN: (Teacher moves or plays rhythm instrument.) Guess who's coming. Daddy? Little brother? Rover? A cow? A pony? A bunny? Etc.

ABOUT MUSICAL GROWTH

Music, we have said, helps children to grow up as persons. The practical meaning of this proposition should be at least fairly clear by now. But a question, and a very proper one, here arises. How much actual music will children learn in the wide, rich, varied pattern of creative activities that have been described and carefully arranged for in this book? What about specific musical growth itself?

One thing is as clear as day. There cannot be much growth *through* music unless there is, at the same time, growth *in* music. Unless children achieve a developing grasp of music itself, musical experiences are not going to do them much good of any kind.

But the converse of this proposition is also abundantly true. Children grow *in* music by just the sort of varied, rich, creative experiences that make music a very valuable influence for personal growth. This can be proved with reference to our book, for it is possible specifically to chart the growing grasp of music that can and should—and, indeed, we might even say *must*—come from the proper use of its materials.

A MUSICAL GROWTH CHART

Classified Indices

RHYTHMIC INDEX

Song Titles

Italics have been used to indicate the page numbers of songs and the first lines of songs.

INDEX OF INSTRUMENTAL MATERIAL